REBUILDING

A LIFE THAT

MATTERS

How You Can
Rise From the Rubble

John Mark Caton, PhD.

Rebuilding a Life That Matters: How You Can Rise From the Rubble
John Mark Caton

Published by Austin Brothers Publishing, Fort Worth, Texas

www.abpbooks.com

ISBN978-1-7359739-4-4

Printed in the United States of America
2021 -- First Edition

This book is dedicated to those in our church,
community, and country who journeyed through
so much this past year. We have experienced
tremendous loss, and many others have navigated
unbelievable hurt and heartache. In times like these
there is only one thing to do—
Rebuild a Life that Matters!

Contents

Introduction

Why We Need to Rebuild

The year 2020 taught us a lot of things, but first among them is that there is A LOT that needs to be rebuilt. A review of this single calendar year reveals a multitude of broken down systems: our economy is struggling, our political culture is bitterly divided, our health care system has been overwhelmed by the COVID-19 pandemic, our educational systems are fraught with inequality and disagreement over whether kids should even *be* in school, our justice system exhibits both deplorable examples of police brutality and passionate calls to defund the police, and our modes of peaceful protest regarding all these things have often degenerated into lawless looting, rioting, and destructive behavior. It is abundantly clear that something is deeply wrong with our society, and it needs to be rebuilt upon much firmer foundations than we currently have.

It is not just our country that needs to be rebuilt, but rather *we* need to be rebuilt. The strains and stresses of our recent past have exposed how in need of help we really are. As just one example, experts have noted that the COVID-19 pandemic has led many to experience "decision fatigue," which is the sense of being overwhelmed at the number of decisions that one must make every day (like whether to wear a mask, eat in a restaurant, etc.). Others have noted that the pandemic has caused a huge rise in mental health conditions like depression and alcoholism. These are just the tip of the iceberg, for the Bible makes it clear that if we take a moment to reflect, we will realize just how broken each and every one of us really is, and how much we stand in need of God's grace.

This book is an attempt to help us, as the people of God, in a much-needed rebuilding effort. My hope is that this book will inspire us to rise from the rubble of our broken lives, shattered dreams, evident failures, and fragmented country. My prayer is that the Lord would use this book to help each of us to rebuild a life that really matters, one that overcomes the difficulties we will inevitably face in this life, and makes a lasting impact for the kingdom of God.

Why Nehemiah is a Great Place to Start Rebuilding

To help us in thinking about what it means to rebuild our lives in the way that God intends, we are going to be looking at the book of Nehemiah in the Bible. Why? Because Nehemiah is all about rebuilding. You see, Nehemiah was an Israelite exile serving as cupbearer to the king of the Persian Empire. The book begins with him learning that the walls of Jerusalem *still* have not been properly rebuilt from the Babylonian attack more than a century earlier. In the ancient world, that was a *huge* problem; there was no way that God's people, who had returned to the Promised Land, could have stability and a functioning temple system to worship God without an intact wall and rebuilt gates. Nehemiah knew that the wall had to be rebuilt, and he knew it would require a great commitment on his part to see that it happened.

Nehemiah is given to us as an example of someone who makes a commitment that makes a big impact. The situation he faces is a picture of our situation: the walls of our country are broken down and, at times, the walls in our lives are broken down. We need to rebuild, to look to the Lord and ask Him to help us rise from the rubble by making commitments that will lead to true change, that will lead to lives that have lasting impact. As we watch what occurs in Nehemiah's time and how the Lord is faithful to his people amidst their distress, we can learn so much about what it might look like to rebuild our lives, our churches, our communities, our country, and even our world. Does that sound too ambitious? It will not if we remember that "it is God who works in you, both to will and to work for his good pleasure" (Philippians 2:13).

In fact, as we look at Nehemiah, we see a basic pattern set out for us in terms of what it looks like to go about rebuilding a life that matters. First, we must *identify the problem*. For Nehemiah, that part was easy. Nehemiah 1:3 says, "They said to me, 'Those who survived the exile and are back in the province are in great trouble and disgrace. The wall of Jerusalem is broken down, and its gates have been burned with fire.'" Nehemiah received an honest report of the problem: the walls were down. What about for you? As you begin this book, you might begin to ask where are your spiritual or physical walls broken down? Where do you need God's help to address problems in your life? Where are you convinced that the work of rebuilding needs to get underway in your life and in your world?

Next in the pattern, we see that we must *pray for success*. Sometimes we think that praying for success is selfish or unspiritual, but Nehemiah prays specifically for success in the rebuilding effort. Look at Nehemiah 1:11: "Lord, let your ear be attentive to the prayer of this your servant and to the prayer of your servants who delight in revering your name. Give your servant success today by granting him favor in the presence of this man." Nehemiah knew that the only way the rebuilding effort was going to be successful was by the grace and greatness of God. When we define success according to God's definition, we realize that praying for this kind of success brings great glory to God because we recognize from the beginning: we cannot do it without Him. We are never going to rise from the rubble with rebuilt lives without God's power at work within us.

But then, finally, we see in the pattern that we must *make commitments that matter*. For Nehemiah, there came a point where he had to commit. He learned about the problem, he prayed, but it came time to act. Look at Nehemiah 2:4-5: "The king said to me, "What is it you want?" Then I prayed to the God of heaven, and I answered the king, "If it pleases the king and if your servant has found favor in his sight, let him send me to the city in Judah where my ancestors are buried so that I can rebuild it."

Since Nehemiah was in a foreign land, serving under a foreign king, he had to seek permission from the king to build the wall. His boldness in asking the king is what set things in motion. Had Nehemiah identified the problem and prayed, but not taken any action, nothing would have happened. But he did act, and he made a commitment to rebuild the wall. This was more than a feeling or even a passionate prayer—it was a commitment to do the work to get the job done. If your life is anything like mine, there have been times when you identified the problem and maybe even prayed for success, but you never ended up acting. The result was no improvement. Therefore, we need to make commitments that matter, so that we are consistently moved to action.

After all, we see in the Bible that there is a close relationship between faith and works. Faith is what saves us, but our works are what keeps us on the path to becoming all that God wants us to be. Nehemiah has faith that God can help him rebuild the walls, but then he made commitments that mattered and put in the work to rebuild the walls. Let us step into this study of Nehemiah and see how his faith and works came together to enable a rebuilding effort to be tremendously successful, and how the same could be true in your own life today, for your good and for God's glory.

Chapter 1: Know Your Vision

Read Nehemiah 1:1-2:20

Big Picture

How do we rebuild a life that matters? First, we need to understand the vision God has for each of our lives that comes through intentionally seeking the Lord in His Word, in prayer, and in community. As we reflect on God's character and promises, we will better know and live into the vision He has for us and for His people all over the world.

Why We Need Vision:

Helen Keller made a profound observation when she said: "The most pathetic person in the world is someone who has sight but has no vision." Jesus Himself spoke in a similar way about people who were "ever seeing but never perceiving" (Matthew 13:14). Indeed, to truly perceive what is happening in our lives and in our world is to go beyond merely "seeing" our external circumstances; it is to understand those circumstances amidst a much bigger picture. This sort of perception is what we might call a "vision" for our lives: the ability to see ourselves in light of something larger than each of us. If we do not have such a vision for our life, it is easy to feel lost, depressed, and purposeless. Proverbs 29:18 even says (in the KJV): "Where there is no vision, the people perish." Vision is so important. It gives us direction, purpose and meaning—a reason to live!

The truth is, all of us have some kind of vision for our life that we follow, something that powerfully guides our long-term priorities and everyday decisions. The question is: what *kind* of vision is currently informing your life? Many of us end up living according to visions that are ultimately very disappointing and thin. For instance, if you are living for a vision that a particular political party will be able to acquire power and change all that is wrong with our country, that vision might feel particularly inadequate when *the other party* wins the election. To rebuild a life that matters, we need a vision that is big enough to guide us through all the ups and downs of life and that endures from our first days to our final breath.

Where We Get Vision:

Where can we go for such a vision? To the One Who created us and knows us in our innermost being (Psalm 139). The Lord is the only One Who can provide a truly satisfying and enduring vision for our lives, one that enables us to ask of whatever circumstances we are in: what is *the Lord* doing, and desiring to do, amidst these? And the wonderful news is that God created us with a purpose. He *has* a vision for our lives, and amazingly, that vision is one that includes specific plans for us, a gracious prospering of us, and a particular hope in us. This is a summary of the promise given in Jeremiah 29:11, "'For I know *the plans I have for you*,' declares the LORD, 'plans to *prosper you* and not to harm you, plans to *give you hope* and a future.'" Let's look at each of these in more detail.

God's vision includes *specific plans* for us. God has a plan for my life, and the more I seek to align my plans with God's plans, the more success and meaning I will have in my daily life—even in the mundane moments. After all, if I believe that God has a specific plan for me, then *everything that occurs* happens for a purpose. If I stumble upon a butterfly at the exact moment it is emerging from its cocoon, I can be assured that the Lord has planned this encounter for me.

While we make lots of plans that do not actually come to pass (as the COVID-19 pandemic has taught us well!), we have the promise in Scripture that the Lord's plans can never falter. It's wonderful to know that, unlike our plans that fail again and again, the Lord's plans never will! This is the promise of Proverbs 19:21, "Many are the plans in a person's heart, but it is the Lord's purpose that prevails."

The apostle James reminds us that when we make plans, we should hold them loosely and always submit them to the Lord's plan (James 4:13-15). And Jesus Himself not only instructs us to pray "not my will, but yours be done" (Matthew 26:39), but also reminds us that God has a plan to care for us, which far surpasses His care for the birds of the air who can do no long-term planning (Matthew 6:25-27). God's plans for us are good plans indeed!

But God's vision also includes *a gracious prospering* of us. When we think of prospering, we too often limit it to money or financial gain. But prospering includes so much more—a stable family, flourishing children, refined character, and impactful legacy come to mind. Prospering in a biblical sense means being aligned with God's design for our world in every aspect of your life. God's vision for us is that we would prosper, that we would be blessed by Him and enjoy the fullness of life.

We see this by directly contrasting God's vision for us with Satan's. Jesus tells us in John 10:10, "The thief comes only to steal and kill and destroy; I have come that they may have life and have it to the full." Jesus wants us to be aware of Satan's scheme to steal from us, kill our dreams, and destroy everything that is important to us. Jesus wants us to have life abundantly, a life and attitude that allows us to enjoy all of God's best as we live with a sense of purpose.

Scripture is full of promises that God desires to graciously prosper us. Consider Deuteronomy 6:24, "The Lord commanded us to obey all these decrees and to fear the Lord our God, so that we might always prosper and be kept alive, as is the case today." Psalm 1:3 reminds us that the righteous person "is like a tree planted by streams of water, which yields its fruit in season and whose leaf does not wither— whatever they do prospers." And Romans 8:28 climaxes Paul's reflection on the Gospel by reminding us that "we know that in all things God works for the good of those who love him, who have been called according to his purpose." God's grace enables us to truly prosper no matter how difficult the circumstance.

Lastly, God's vision includes *a particular hope* in us. Biblical hope is not like "hoping" your favorite NFL team will win the Super Bowl; rather, it is a confident assurance of a future grace. Through the years I have found the acronym *HOPE,* helpful in envisioning what it looks like to have hope within us because of what God has promised. First, *'H'* – *'Hang on to God's Promises.'* There are many promises in Scripture for God's people to hang on to regardless of how tough or confusing the circumstances. One of them is 1 Peter 1:3: "Praise be to the God and Father of our Lord Jesus Christ! In his great mercy he has given us new birth into a living hope through the resurrection of Jesus Christ from the dead."

Next is *'O'—'Overcome Life's Obstacles.'* Going through tough times or circumstances is not incompatible with living a prosperous life, assuming our definition of prospering is biblical. When Paul says in Romans 15:13, "May the God of hope fill you with all joy and peace as you trust in him, so that you may overflow with hope by the power of the Holy Spirit," he did not have a limit on when and how we could experience that joy and peace.

Next is *'P'* – *'Pursue God's Will.'* Too often, we find ourselves pursuing our will and our plans over God's. However, Paul tells us in Titus 2:12-14, God's grace changes that by teaching us "to say 'No' to ungodliness and worldly passions, and to live self-controlled, upright and godly lives in this present age, while we wait for the blessed hope—the appearing of the glory of our great God and Savior, Jesus Christ, Who gave himself for us to redeem us from all wickedness and to purify for himself a people that are his very own, eager to do what is good."

Lastly, there is *'E'* – *'Expect God to do something amazing.'* Living with expectancy creates a child-like faith as to what God is going to do next. God does not always do the amazing according to our time or even in our way, but as His people we know He is up to something good. In this we take our cue from Habakkuk 1:5, "Look at the nations and watch— and be utterly amazed. For I am going to do something in your days that you would not believe, even if you were told."

Now this is a vision for life worth following! We all long to live a life that is purposeful and satisfying? Well, by turning to and trusting in the One Who has made us and given us these very precious promises in Scripture, we embrace *His* vision for our lives with its specific plans for us, its gracious prospering of us, and its hope in us. In Ephesians 3:20-21 Paul says, "Now to him who is able to do immeasurably more than all we ask or imagine, according to his power that is at work within us, to him be glory in the church and in Christ Jesus throughout all generations, for ever and ever! Amen." Paul reminds us here that God's vision for our life includes more than we could ever ask or imagine. In other words, Paul says that if I follow any other vision for life, even if it includes all the things I would ever need and want, I would *still* be missing out because that vision pales in comparison to all that God has planned for us.

If we find ourselves having small dreams and small goals, that may be an indication that God is playing a small role in our thinking. By contrast, God's vision for our life allows us to plan big and dream bigger than we ever thought possible. It is that vision we are seeking to recapture to rebuild our lives around His purposes for us.

In the following pages we are going to look at how Nehemiah is an example given to us in Scripture of someone who knew God's vision for his life and pressed into that vision amidst the difficult circumstances he and his people faced. Indeed, what we will find is that knowing the character and promises of God allowed him to respond to a very dire situation, providing us an example to follow and encouraging us that no matter how difficult life may be for you right now, there is hope!

Nehemiah knew God's vision for his life. So, when he was faced with horrendous circumstances and the prospect of having to rebuild from the rubble, he drew upon that vision to

1. Identify the problem
2. Be honest about past failures
3. Take some risk
4. Solidify a plan
5. Solve the problem

Let us look at each of these in more detail.

1. Identify the Problem

Nehemiah 1:2-4, "Hanani, one of my brothers, came from Ju-dah with some other men, and I questioned them about the Jewish remnant that had survived the exile, and also about Jerusalem. They said to me, "Those who survived the exile and are back in the province are in great trouble and disgrace. The wall of Jerusalem is broken down, and its gates have been burned with fire." When I heard these things, I sat down and wept..."

We see here that one of the first steps toward knowing and realigning your life to God's vision is to first identify the problems in and around you. We are only going to make progress toward God's vision for our lives if we are willing to take an honest inventory of our problems—and we all have them. Being able to identify these problems accurately and honestly is essential in aligning with God's vision for your life, but too often we do not invest the time and energy to take stock of our life's troubles in the way we need to. You might say that the first step in rebuilding your life is to *slow down* enough to ask the question: where are things in my life that are clearly out of alignment with God's good plan and purpose?

What is the problem at the beginning of the book of Ne-hemiah? We might be tempted to identify it as the fact that the people in Jerusalem were in great trouble and disgrace. A closer examination leads us to see that great trouble and disgrace were the *result* of the problem, but not the problem itself. The problem was that, as Nehemiah 1:3 notes, "the wall of Jerusalem is broken down." The result of the wall being down is that the people were struggling and hopeless, especially because in that day the security of a city was dependent on whether there was a fortification of some kind to protect it.

This following is what two biblical scholars say about the problem Nehemiah was dealing with: "For a city to be without a good wall on an ongoing basis was unthinkable in the ancient Near East, since it was actually the principal element in a city's defense. If the wall was broken down, the city was vulnerable to attack, and this was a source of shame to the city's residents. This explains Nehemiah's reaction when he hears about the state of Jerusalem's wall. The possibility of further attack and destruction and the associated shame experienced by the Judeans were the opposite of the peace and security associated with restoration. Thus, Nehemiah perceives a need for further action by God to fulfill his promises."[1]

It is only when Nehemiah has really been able to identify the problem that he can understand the inevitable results and develop a plan of action to address the problem. If Nehemiah had not taken the time to inquire about the state of his people in Jerusalem, he might not have ever learned about this dire need. But Nehemiah demonstrates the good that can come when we *slow down* to take stock of the problems in our lives and in our world. And, as we will see, he also embodies the proper response of lament regarding the horrific situation and of action in seeking to remedy it.

This part of Nehemiah's story is particularly instructive for us in two ways. First, it teaches us that we need to make sure we do not *misidentify* the problems in our lives and in the lives of others. It is so easy to confuse the *results* of the problem with the underlying *problem itself*. If your marriage is struggling—that is the result of some underlying problems, but it is not the problem itself. The problem may be poor communication or being unkind

---

1   Douglas J. E. Nykolaishen and Andrew J. Schmutzer, *Ezra, Nehemiah, and Esther*, a vol. in *Teach the Text Commentary Series*, ed. Mark L. Strauss and John H. Walton (Grand Rapids, MI: Baker Books, 2018), 104.

or being unwilling to forgive. *These* are the problems—and the result is that your marriage is struggling. Or consider the difficulty of being buried under financial debt; this may be the result of an underlying problem of financial mismanagement. It is only when you have identified the problem itself that you can focus on fixing it.

If we focus on the wrong things or fail to differentiate between problems and results, we will be ineffective at fulfilling God's vision for our lives, and we will be equally ineffective at helping others fulfill God's vision for their lives. Being able to properly identify problems is the first step to fulfilling God's vision for your life. Consider taking some time, even right now, to get honest and specific about the problems that you are facing in your life now. Write them down and acknowledge them before the Lord who is powerful enough to help you overcome them.

But this part of Nehemiah's story is also instructive in helping us recognize that no problem, however pervasive and overwhelming, is too great for our God. It cannot be stressed enough that Nehemiah lived in perhaps the lowest point of Israel's history. Due to their own sin and unwillingness to repent, God had raised up enemies who had not only removed them from their homeland but tore down the most important aspects of their way of life (e.g., the temple). Yet, it is in the midst of the rubble that God was still working His purposes and His vision for His people.

Nehemiah found himself being used as an instrument of the rebuilding process of God. God is not surprised or overwhelmed by the rubble, but often glorifies Himself by meeting us in the midst of the rubble and promising to be strong for us. If you are reading this and you feel as if your life, and perhaps the life of your church, community, and nation is a mess—then, the book of Nehemiah has good news for you. It reminds us that no situation is too difficult for God to overcome and redeem. God's vision for our prosperity is always toward restoration and rebuilding, even when we hit rock bottom. As Christians we can look squarely at the problems we face and know that the Lord is not intimidated by them, so, neither should we be.

2. Be Honest about Past Failures

Nehemiah 1:4-7, "...For some days I mourned and fasted and prayed before the God of heaven. Then I said: "LORD, the God of heaven, the great and awesome God, who keeps his covenant of love with those who love him and keep his commandments, let your ear be attentive and your eyes open to hear the prayer your servant is praying before you day and night for your servants, the people of Israel. I confess the sins we Israelites, including myself and my father's family, have committed against you. We have acted very wickedly toward you. We have not obeyed the commands, decrees and laws you gave your servant Moses."

One of the biggest hurdles of knowing and aligning with God's vision for us is a failure to grapple with the past failures of our lives. This goes beyond just identifying the current problems we face; it moves to a place of honest recognition of how we got to this place, which often involves patterns of sin and rebellion that we have committed or that have been committed against us. Until we have come to grips with these past failures and how they have negatively impacted who we are, we will never *really* be able to address the problems in our lives. We see that confession of our sins and an honest recognition of where we have fallen short of God's vision for our lives is also a vital first step toward healing and wholeness.

Did you see that this is exactly what Nehemiah did here? When he heard about the devastating situation that his fellow

Israelites were in, he did not begin the *blame game* and start pointing fingers at others (like the Babylonians who had originally knocked down the wall and taken them captive). His response is to mourn, fast, and pray to God, to get reoriented as he grapples with this horrific situation. And then he rehearses God's good promises to his people: the Lord rules from Heaven, is great and powerful beyond measure, keeps His covenant with those who love Him, and is attentive to the prayers of His people. When he remembers who God is, he is better able to see who *He* is and who *His people* are: sinners who have acted wickedly and not obeyed the commands God had given to Israel.

It is important to notice that Nehemiah confessed his own sins but also confessed the sins of his people. When acknowledging past failures, Nehemiah did not merely run down his own personal list if sins; he included himself among God's people who had failed in spectacular ways over the course of Israel's history. Nehemiah recognized that their story was his story, that their past failures were, in a way, his past failures. He sees clearly that we are not islands unto ourselves. Rather, we are impacted by the sins and failures of others, and this inevitably determines the kinds of problems that we will have in life. Nehemiah realizes that bringing all this before the Lord in humble confession is one of the most important things he can do if the problems that his people face are ever going to be overcome.

At this point we can see two more areas where Nehemiah's story is instructive for us. First, we need to understand that past failures, while they have impacted us, do not need to define us. It is rightly said that failure is an event, but it cannot be a person. If we are honest about our failures and learn from our mistakes, our failures ultimately become part of our journey to success. The *secret sauce of life* is not living a fail-proof life; there is no such thing. Rather, the secret to a successful life is not being defined by those past failures and instead using them as motivation for change. Winston Churchill once said that success is going from failure to failure without losing enthusiasm. The reason we do not have to lose enthusiasm for pursuing God's vision amidst all the failures of our lives is that these failures do not define us. Why not? Because God has graciously promised to help us and heal us and make us more and more like Jesus. Though all of us (and I am at the front of the line!) have failed in many ways and at many times—the grace of God to forgive and renew is much bigger than all those failures. Maybe you are reading this book right now, remembering your past failures, and wondering if God can ever use you again. The answer, friend, is that He absolutely can, and Nehemiah is going to be a wonderful example of that for you.

The second thing we learn from Nehemiah at this point is that honesty is key. If we are not honest about our sin and the past failures of our lives, we can never fully leave them behind and set our eyes on what is ahead. Confession of our sin, and an acknowledgement of how the community around us has sinned as well, is a key ingredient in realigning with God's vision and beginning to rebuild your life from the rubble. In order to move forward and begin addressing the problems in our lives, we have to begin with an honest assessment of who we are (in all our brokenness) so we can be surrendered to God's purpose for who He wants us to be. As we serve God and seek to achieve great things for Him, God has a much bigger goal in mind: working on you amidst this whole process! Be honest about your past failures and your need before God. Be willing to learn from your mistakes. This is critical for you to be willing to take some risks for God as you rebuild your life.

3. Take Some Risk

Nehemiah 2:1-2, "…when wine was brought for him, I took the wine and gave it to the king. I had not been sad in his presence before, so the king asked me, "Why does your face look so sad when you are not ill? This can be nothing but sadness of heart." I was very much afraid…"

Nehemiah 2:10, "When Sanballat the Horonite and Tobiah the Ammonite official heard about this, they were very much disturbed that someone had come to promote the welfare of the Israelites."

Nehemiah 2:20,"I answered them by saying, "The God of heaven will give us success. We his servants will start rebuilding…"

Knowing and realigning your life with God's vision is going to involve taking risks. Why? Because you will be doing new things, things that your previous vision for life did not ask you to do. Taking risks is one of the ways we know that we are trusting God, and not ourselves, for a prospering life. Anytime we take on something new, there is a little bit of risk involved. Letting a sixteen-year-old behind the wheel is a risk, but it is an essential risk if they are ever going to become a competent, independent driver. Risks can be small (risking rejection by asking if someone would be willing to join you for Bible study once a week) or they can be large (cashing in your 401k out of the conviction that the money would be better spent on world mission efforts), but either way, they involve the same dimension: having to trust God for something new and something that makes you more vulnerable.

Nehemiah was the cupbearer to the king. That was no small thing in that day and age—it was a lofty position inside a pagan king's house, primarily because one of the cupbearer's responsibilities was to make sure the king had wine and that the wine was not poisoned! This position meant Nehemiah was in the presence of the king regularly, and it was expected that Nehemiah would not show any displeasure or sadness in the king's presence. In fact, in those days being sad in the King's presence could get you fired or even worse—it could cost you your life. However, Nehemiah realized that the problem facing his people was too great and that he had to be honest with the king by being visibly sad in his presence. This was a risk! But Nehemiah took a step of faith and trusted God amidst that risk.

As Nehemiah returns to Jerusalem, we see another risk that he had to take. The people which surrounded Jerusalem were not pleased at all that any effort would be made to help the city become reestablished. In fact, they had incentive to see that the city *did not* become reestablished, so much so that they were willing to harass and even attack those who would try to rebuild it. These nations and their leaders were the ones who had power in the region: financial power, military power, social power. So, Nehemiah risked his life and the lives of his people by undertaking a rebuilding effort. At the end of chapter 2, he makes it clear what enables him to take that risk: he knows that his God is big enough to protect them and give them success.

At this point in the story there are two more things we need to note. The first is that we need to be honest about the fact that choosing to align with God's vision for your life is risky business. I know for me, when I think back to the twenty-five years I have served as the Pastor at Cottonwood Creek, we have had to take some huge risks as a church to follow the vision that the Lord had for us. And so, as the church's Pastor, it means that I had to take some large personal risks as well. There were times when I was afraid to take the risk because I was afraid the effort would fail. But amazingly, every time our church took a great risk for

God that we were certain He wanted us to take, we succeeded. This has taught me that it is always better taking a risk for God than regretting that you did not for the rest of your life. If you take a risk and it pays off, you will be happier and more fulfilled. If it does not pay off, you will be wiser for having tried. In short, taking risks comes with the territory of realigning your life with God's vision for it.

The second thing is that we need to see that taking a risk with God at the helm is actually no risk at all. Yes, Nehemiah's earthly circumstances made it seem like this was a very bad idea; being sad in the king's presence and upsetting regional enemies was a good way to end up dead! But Nehemiah trusted God and knew that God was powerful enough to overcome these obstacles in ways that he could not in his own strength. The risk was made void by the power of God, who could supply all the protection and resources he would need to solve the problem.

Nehemiah understood that God was present every step of the risky endeavor, and we need to recognize this is no less true for Christians today. If God approves of something, then no enemy or circumstance will be able to stand in the way of its completion. Our call is to trust and obey, even if, in the world's eyes, it is a foolish endeavor. In fact, one of the ways we know we are on the right path to realigning our lives to God's vision for it is whether we are setting goals that require God to come through for us. If we are not taking any risks, it might be exposing the fact that we are not relying on God in the way we should be in our daily lives and in our long-term planning.

4. Solidify a Plan

Nehemiah 1:8-11, "Remember the instruction you gave your servant Moses, saying, 'If you are unfaithful, I will scatter you among the nations, but if you return to me and obey my commands, then even if your exiled people are at the farthest horizon, I will gather them from there and bring them to the place I have chosen as a dwelling for my Name.' "They are your servants and your people, whom you redeemed by your great strength and your mighty hand. Lord, let your ear be attentive to the prayer of this your servant and to the prayer of your servants who delight in revering your name. Give your servant success today by granting him favor in the presence of this man."

Nehemiah 2:4-5, "The king said to me, "What is it you want?" Then I prayed to the God of heaven, and I answered the king, "If it pleases the king and if your servant has found favor in his sight, let him send me to the city in Judah where my ancestors are buried so that I can rebuild it."

It is important to understand that taking risks does not mean acting without a plan. In fact, taking risks without a plan is quite foolish. Taking risks wisely means fully counting the cost and preparing in all the ways that will bring success to the risky endeavor. Jesus Himself reminds us of the importance of such planning when He points out the foolishness of constructing a building or planning to attack an enemy without first assessing whether one has the proper resources to succeed at the task (Luke 14:28-33). Realigning your life with God's vision for it will require quite a bit of preparation and planning. We might say that life change is a long-term project, and as we all know, the only way long-term projects are successful is with careful planning.

Part of that planning for Nehemiah involved prayer, for praying is the best preparation that one can do in beginning to solve a problem. It acknowledges from the beginning that there is only One Person Who can really help: God Himself. Nehemiah prays to God, and he does so by rehearsing in his prayer God's own promise to help His people if they return to Him and obey His commands. Nehemiah intentionally reorients his perspective by remembering what God has said in His Word and then making petition in light of that Word in prayer.

Nehemiah not only prayed, but he made the preparations that would be necessary if and when his prayer was answered. Ultimately, after much prayer and fasting, Nehemiah still had to open his mouth and ask the Persian king for permission to leave his position and return to Jerusalem with the king's resources in order to rebuild the wall. This was after some time of planning, assessing that this was the best way forward despite the risks. Nehemiah also knew that he would have to ask the king for certain supplies and permissions and had a very intentional plan for doing so, once he got the king's permission to return. Nehemiah did not just venture out on this risky endeavor; he patiently waited and planned for success.

At this point we can note two important takeaways for us. The first is that we must plan but not get bogged down in the details of the plan. It has been said many times over that failing to plan is planning to fail. Some of my greatest failures have come because I simply failed to plan. Nehemiah is a great reminder that we must plan but be willing to adjust the plan as we go.

Nehemiah's initial plan was simple: he was going to rebuild the wall. At this point, Nehemiah does not have all the details. He does not have the manpower or the design yet, but he does have a plan. Part of what makes this plan so effective at first is that it was simple. Too often, we spend so much time planning and optimizing that we get bogged down in looking for the very best solution to our problem.

When seeking God's will for your life, your plan needs to stay simple. You only need to answer these two questions: What does God want me to do? and What is the first step toward implementing that? Plan but know that the details will work themselves out. Even the best plan in our mind might fail when it is put into practice. But do not ever forget—if plan *A* does not work, there are 25 other letters in the alphabet.

The second take away is to never overestimate the importance of prayer in establishing a plan. How foolish it is to rush into action without first going before the One Who has the power to give our endeavors success. Nehemiah spent several days mourning, fasting, and praying before he started to plan how he would solve the problem. This was not wasted time; this was very well invested time. By remembering the promises God had made to his people, and by asking God to bless his endeavor in light of those promises, Nehemiah took the most important step toward ensuring his plan's success. This is because he knew the truth of Proverbs 21:1, "In the Lord's hand the king's heart is a stream of water that he channels toward all who please him."

5. Solve the Problem

Nehemiah 2:6, "Then the king, with the queen sitting beside him, asked me, "How long will your journey take, and when will you get back?" It pleased the king to send me; so I set a time."

Nehemiah 2:11-12, "I went to Jerusalem, and after staying there three days I set out during the night with a few others..."

Nehemiah 2:17-18, "Then I said to them, "You see the trouble we are in: Jerusalem lies in ruins, and its gates have been burned with fire. Come, let us rebuild the wall of Jerusalem, and we will no longer be in disgrace." I also told them about the gracious hand of my God on me and what the king had said to me. They replied, "Let us start rebuilding." So they began this good work."

At some point, we must get moving! Solidifying a plan is the first step toward solving a problem, but the problem does not get solved by planning alone. We must implement the plan, taking initiative to set the gears in motion. As important as prayer and preparation is, we know that obtaining God's approval and power does not negate the individual's responsibility to act. A prayer and a plan are not sufficient to accomplish a task. Completion requires a willingness to make progress toward solving the problem.

Nehemiah begins to act the moment he opens his mouth and asks the king for permission. He takes another practical step by setting a date for the journey. Another step involves making the appropriate arrangements for the travel and rebuilding. Yet another step came in making the trip to Jerusalem, and this was followed closely by his surveying of the wall (at night: he needed to be secret about his plans because of the opposition that he would face from neighboring nations). But even at this point, this has all been preparation for the actual work of rebuilding the wall. Nehemiah understands that *this* is the work that needs to get underway after all the careful planning and preparation, so he draws the people together to announce his plan and they finally get to work rebuilding! The rest of the book of Nehemiah will be exploring what happened as this rebuilding project moved to completion.

But for now, two more things for us to learn from this portion of Nehemiah's story. The first is that if we are going to know and fulfill God's vision for our lives, there must be a starting point. We can identify problems, acknowledge past failures, initiate risks, and solidify plans all we want, but until we take action, these will all just be tune-ups in the garage. At some point, you must turn on the engine and get the car on the road. This is because a plan, however good, without action is just a dream.

My wife Jeana reminds our children of this when they come to her with a problem they are facing. She reminds them in a simple statement, "solve your problem." Half the battle of solving a problem is just getting started to solve it. Nehemiah wisely set a time to get started, and he followed his timeline; he acted when the time came rather than procrastinating out of fear or laziness. We need to learn to do the same rather than being so quick to say, "I'll get around to it." The truth is that is a great way to never get around to something the Lord is calling you to do. Is today the day to set a time and get started on that venture?

The second thing we need to see is that there are going to be many reasons to not begin the work. Think about all the reasons Nehemiah had to not take on the task of rebuilding the wall: he had a comfortable job in the palace where he had abundant provision, and this meant risking a good relationship with the king and launching out into an environment full of dangers to reestablish a city he was not even going to live in. But Nehemiah had a larger vision to motivate him, one that was based on God's promises found in His Word.

It is only that reorientation that is going to enable us to overcome the temptations to remain in the status quo. Is something holding you back from getting started in realigning with God's vision for your life? Are you too busy or distracted? Are you fearful of failure? Let the promises that we find in Scripture help you overcome those excuses and accept the invitation that God is offering to you right now to join Him on mission in this world. God is inviting you to something bigger and better than what you have been doing. Ask God right now what He wants you to do—then start doing that!

Next Steps

We have seen how Nehemiah chapters 1-2 issues a call for us to know our vision, to know the vision that God has for our lives which includes specific plans for us, a gracious prospering of us, and a particular hope in us. When we are living out of that vision, we can do what Nehemiah did: identify the problems in our lives, acknowledge past failures, initiate risks, solidify plans, and then actually solve those problems. This is one vital part of how we rebuild a life that matters. And so, as we leave this chapter, it is important to think about what commitments you might need to make to grow in this. We have said that part of how we better understand the vision God has for each of our lives comes through intentionally seeking the Lord in His Word, in prayer, and in community. In light of that, I'd like to offer five potential commitments you could make to grow in this over the course of our study:

1. Commit to Read God's Word

Nehemiah 9:3, "They stood where they were and read from the Book of the Law of the LORD their God for a quarter of the day, and spent another quarter in confession and in worshiping the LORD their God."

2. Commit to Corporate Worship

Nehemiah 12:27, "At the dedication of the wall of Jerusalem, the Levites were sought out from where they lived and were brought to Jerusalem to celebrate joyfully the dedication with songs of thanksgiving and with the music of cymbals, harps and lyres."

3. Commit to Join a Small Group

Nehemiah 3:1-3, "Eliashib the high priest and his fellow priests went to work and rebuilt the Sheep Gate... The men of Jericho built the adjoining section, and Zakkur son of Imri built next to them. The Fish Gate was rebuilt by the sons of Hassenaah."

4. Commit to Serve Others

Nehemiah 6:15-16, "So the wall was completed... in fifty-two days. When all our enemies heard about this, all the surrounding nations were afraid and lost their self-confidence, because they realized that this work had been done with the help of our God."

5. Commit to Pray Daily

Nehemiah 2:4, "...Then I prayed to the God of heaven."

Prayer: Lord, help me to know which of these commitments are the most important for me to grow in better understanding, and living into, the vision You have for my life. I surrender to You and Your plans for my life, which are much better than any plans I could make. I trust You and ask You to do a deep work of transformation and renewal in me as we go about this study of how to rebuild our lives according to Your design. May I have a soft heart to sense Your leading and bold hands to get to the work you are calling me to do. In Jesus' name I pray... Amen.

Chapter 2: Know Your Place

Read Nehemiah 3:1-32

Big Picture

How do we rebuild a life that matters? After we have come to grasp the vision God has for each of our lives, we need to know what role the Lord would have us play in His kingdom work. Each of us has a vital role to play in that work, and today that means each of us brings certain gifts and graces to the church to better accomplish its mission. Recognizing this and serving in places where we contribute those gifts and graces helps each of us see how our lives matter to God and to His people. A place to serve in the kingdom helps us rise from the rubble.

A Place in God's Kingdom

So far, we have talked about the importance of making commitments that realign with God's vision for our lives as a critical part of rebuilding a life that matters. The next step is knowing your place in God's work, understanding that He has a critical role for you to play in what He is up to in the world through the church.

We all know what it is like to feel "out of place," being in a situation where you do not feel comfortable or get the sense that you do not belong. Sometimes we feel out of place in our jobs, sometimes in our neighborhoods, and sometimes even in our own families. At times, this is nothing more than a *feeling*, something you sense to be true, but which does not align with reality. But other times, it is a *fact*, a hard truth that you are out of sync with those around you and maybe do not even have a place there at all. An unshaven cowboy does not just *feel* out of place in a sparkling country club; he *is* out of place.

Scripture promises that if we are Christ followers, we are going to be different from the world, out of place within it to some extent. For instance, Jesus says in John 15:19, "If you belonged to the world, it would love you as its own. As it is, you do not belong to the world, but I have chosen you out of the world. That is why the world hates you." Paul teaches in Romans 12:2 that we should "not conform to the pattern of this world but be transformed by the renewing of your mind. Then you will be able to test and approve what God's will is—his good, pleasing and perfect will." Becoming a Christian means that we no longer have a place in the world in the way we once did.

But the incredible truth is that once we become Christians, we find our *ultimate* place in God's kingdom. For the first time in our lives, we have a family to which we will always belong. That family is the community of faith; that place is the church. In God's kingdom we all have a place—and it is "your" place. God has specifically designed that place for you—and finding that place in God's work is one of the most important steps to living a life that is completely satisfied and fulfilled.

Finding Our Place in God's Kingdom

The book of Nehemiah can once again be a huge help to us in envisioning what it means to find our place in God's kingdom work. As we saw in the last chapter, Nehemiah was called to go back to Jerusalem and assist in the vital task of rebuilding Jerusalem's gates, something that needed to be done if the city were to ever flourish again. The task before him was great: the wall had been down for over 140 years and was in great disrepair. Nehemiah knew he could not rebuild it all by himself. He needed all of God's people to take their place and rebuild.

In Nehemiah chapter 3, we behold the diversity of people who were engaged in this task. The Hebrew word *hazaq*, which means to repair, rebuild, or work on, is used 34 times in this chapter to remind us that all these different people, in one way or another, were a part of the rebuilding project. They all had a place in the project, and it pictures the fact that each of us has a role to play in the work God has for His people today. For the church to accomplish all that God wants us to accomplish, it is vital that each of us knows our place and begins to serve there!

The chapter provides us a map of sorts, working all the way around the gate and highlighting specific areas that needed to be worked on and how that work was divided up among the people. As one Bible scholar explains, this chapter "describes how Nehemiah effectively organized work crews to repair sections of the city wall, beginning at the Sheep Gate in the north and proceeding in a counter-clockwise direction for the mile and a half circuit of the wall." [2] If we don't get bogged down in trying to pronounce the names (they're tough for me even as a teacher of God's Word!), we

---

2   Edwin M. Yamauchi, "Ezra and Nehemiah," pages 394–467 in *Zondervan Illustrated Bible Backgrounds Commentary*, vol. 3, ed. John W. Walton (Grand Rapids, MI: Zondervan, 2009), 429.

notice all the different places where people work and the diversity of tasks they were engaged in. Each part was vital to the ultimate success of the project.

And we know that the project was *indeed* successful. Nehemiah 6:15-16 informs us that "the wall was completed on the twenty-fifth of Elul, in fifty-two days. When all our enemies heard about this, all the surrounding nations were afraid and lost their self-confidence, because they realized that this work had been done with the help of our God." In just *52 days* (an amazing feat given both the length and necessary thickness of this wall) the miracle of rebuilding took place. But it only happened because 1. God was with His people, 2. They had a faithful and effective leader in Nehemiah, and 3. Everyone knew their place and did the work assigned to them.

The significance of this chapter involves much more than just rebuilding some walls. Indeed, I agree that "Nehemiah 3 should be seen not as merely a list of people involved in a mundane project but as a record of those involved in fulfilling God's promises on earth."[3] When we all know our place in God's kingdom and do the work assigned to us, we can be assured that God's work will be successful. God can and will accomplish His will, but He wants to do it through each of us! Which means we need to consider how we find our place in God's kingdom work, and what we should do once we have found that place. Let us look at *five principles* we see in the text that help us to find our place and orient us in our kingdom service.

---

3   Douglas J. E. Nykolaishen and Andrew J. Schmutzer, Ezra, Nehemiah, and Esther, a vol. in Teach the Text Commentary Series, ed. Mark L. Strauss and John H. Walton (Grand Rapids, MI: Baker Books, 2018), 123.

1. All Had a Place

Nehemiah 2:16-18, "The officials did not know where I had gone or what I was doing, because as yet I had said nothing to the Jews or the priests or nobles or officials or any others who would be doing the work. Then I said to them, "You see the trouble we are in: Jerusalem lies in ruins, and its gates have been burned with fire. Come, let us rebuild the wall of Jerusalem, and we will no longer be in disgrace." I also told them about the gracious hand of my God on me and what the king had said to me. They replied, "Let us start rebuilding." So they began this good work."

God created each of us to be in relationship with others, to work alongside them for a purpose. He did not create us to be "lone rangers," doing everything on our own and acting as if we don't need anyone else. That may be an American ideal, but it is not a biblical one! Instead, Scripture continually shows that we need others, and that God has made us in His image to find our place alongside others in His kingdom. While there are times we must go it alone, most of our lives should be spent in a group. We function better in a group and God's work is best accomplished in a group.

Nehemiah was a leader who understood this. He looked at the dilapidated wall and the work to be done and quickly decided the best way to accomplish the great task of rebuilding was to divide the wall up into sections and let each section be worked on by various groups. Notice the "them" and "us" of Nehemiah 2:16-18: this was a group project for sure!

While we are sometimes tempted to skip over passages in the Bible like Nehemiah chapter 3 that give us a list of names (we might be particularly tempted to skip over the many genealogies that the Bible has, though these serve a purpose too!), this passage is a vital one for understanding the message of the book. If we give this passage a chance and slow down to dig into the list a little bit, some clear patterns emerge. In fact, even a quick reading of Nehemiah 3 will cause us to take notice of two words. Those two words are "next to." While on their own these words are not all that significant, the fact that they are repeated some fifteen times to describe how the people worked "next to" each other clearly communicates the fact that this was a group effort. They did not work in the same place, but they never worked alone.

In fact, the work of rebuilding the wall around Jerusalem was divided into approximately 40 sections and many gates, and this work was completed by groups of people from different places, occupations, and backgrounds. Some of the groups were identified by geography—people from Jericho, Tekoa, etc. Other groups were identified by their vocation—goldsmiths, perfumers, merchants, guards, etc. Still other groups were based on civil roles—rulers of districts, mayors, regional priests, etc. Some groups served with their families while others were composed of singles. As you read Nehemiah 3, there is cause for joy, enthusiasm, and excitement as group after group and person after person take their place of service on the wall. Young, old, single, married, sons, daughters—all show that the beauty of doing God's work unites them amidst their differences. They all had a sense of dedication to doing God's work and rebuilding the wall, bringing their distinct gifts and graces to the task.

So, as you think about your place in God's kingdom and in His church, I want to encourage you to find your group. We know that all believers are "one in Christ Jesus" (Galatians 3:28), but this does not do away with the distinctions between us. You come from a certain place, have a certain occupation, and you have a certain marital status, etc. This passage encourages us to see that you have a place in the church. So... find that place! The picture here is that service is only going to really happen when you find your group to serve with, a group where you share some of these common threads. The church is not a place for a "one-man band:" it is much more a place for playing in a band, or better yet, an entire orchestra. God has specifically gifted and equipped each one of His people in a slightly different way, to serve in a unique way that no one else can. And although God can accomplish His purposes without us, the wonderful blessing is that He invites us into His kingdom work to play a unique role. Have you found that role? If you find a group to serve with, you likely will!

The other thing to take away here is when we serve in groups, they can help us to stay motivated when we need it. Think about how exhausting the rebuilding project would get at, say, day 20 or day 40! We all need a group to keep us going, to be the ones who *provide* the motivation at one point and to be the ones who *need* the motivation at another. The New Testament calls us to "Carry each other's burdens, and in this way, you will fulfill the law of Christ" (Galatians 6:2). This assumes that we will know one another and work with one another so we would know what those burdens might be! Knowing your place necessarily involves finding a group that you can do life and ministry with as you serve God together, motivating one another to continue the work all the way to glory.

2. *Some Served Where They Had a Vested Interest*

Nehemiah 3:1, "Eliashib the high priest and his fellow priests went to work and rebuilt the Sheep Gate. They dedicated it and set its doors in place, building as far as the Tower of the Hundred, which they dedicated, and as far as the Tower of Hananel."

Nehemiah 3:10, "Adjoining this, Jedaiah son of Harumaph made repairs opposite his house…"

Nehemiah 3:12, "Shallum son of Hallohesh, ruler of a half-district of Jerusalem, repaired the next section with the help of his daughters."

The fact is, we all serve more zealously when we have "skin in the game." Skin in the game means that we will be immediately affected by the outcome of whatever endeavor is being undertaken. This is why people who are serious about a new business venture are asked to invest their own money to see that it is successful; or why a whole neighborhood might chip in to repaint a mural on a prominent building that everyone can see.

In Nehemiah 3, we see many people serving in areas of vested interest. We begin by seeing that the priests were the ones who worked to rebuild the sheep gate. Why would they be the ones to rebuild that specific gate? Because the sheep gate was adjacent to the sheep market where temple sacrifices were bought and sold so that Israelites could contribute to and participate in worship. Thus, the priests had a vested interest in rebuilding this gate because they wanted to see the sacrificial system of the temple running in a way that was honoring to God (and enabled their job to be a lot more fulfilling). The fact that the passage begins by recounting the work of the priests (including the high priest) in rebuilding the wall and dedicating their work unto the Lord "contributes further to the impression that there was spiritual significance involved."[4]

But other groups with vested interests are mentioned as well. We are told in verse 10 that Jedaiah made repairs on the portion of the wall next to his family's house. Why? Because if you or I were

---

4   Nykolaishen and Schmutzer, *Ezra, Nehemiah, and Esther*, 125.

asked to rebuild a defensive wall next to our houses (especially if we had reason to think that our houses might be attacked), we would want to do a good job, right? This was the security system of their day, and they wanted it to work!

They had a personal interest in keeping their family safe and protected. This is probably why we are told that Shallum rebuilt a portion of the wall with his daughters (strong daughters no doubt!); they are working together as a family to protect what is theirs, and parents had a vested interest to do this work both with their children and for them (after all, they hoped their homes and land would be passed on intact to the next generation). We see lots of examples of some sort of vested interest throughout the passage: verses 23, 28, 29, and 30 all mention building efforts done by people in front of their own living quarters.

I think this is important to recognize because some times, in the church, we have the idea that serving out of a vested interest is wrong; that if I stand to benefit in any way from the work that I am doing or the volunteer effort I join, that somehow it does not count. And while we would want to be wary of any motivation to serve that was completely self-oriented (with a selfish motivation), we need to see here that the Bible commends vested interest as a motivation for serving in God's kingdom.

As you think about finding your place to serve in the church—do not neglect the obvious. Where do you have a personal interest? For instance, if you have children or students-- have you considered working in the Children or Student Ministry, helping to cultivate an environment where your own kids will flourish in ways that you desire? If you are a single person—have you considered serving in the church in a way that may help you develop deeper relationships within the church? If you are married—have you considered leading the next marriage retreat that you and your spouse might also benefit from? If you are looking for a place to serve and grow in, do not neglect looking at areas of personal interest.

This relates to another important point we see emerge in this passage: Christians should avoid seeing their role in God's kingdom as lesser (or greater) than other roles. It is easy to think that work on the "sheep gate" or the "fountain gate" was the more important role, but the reality is that if the whole wall was not intact, then all of Jerusalem was in trouble. Today, we may find ourselves thinking that evangelism or caring for the poor is the most vital work, and that ushering or serving coffee at the fellowship time are less significant. Nothing could be further from the truth. If you have an interest in serving coffee (maybe you love coffee and it brings you great delight to see other people delighting in it), then serve coffee to the glory of God. Your area of interest is one that you should aspire to do with a heart to honor God and build others up. This is one of the most essential steps in serving well in God's kingdom.

3. Some Served for the Benefit of Others

Nehemiah 3:2, "The men of Jericho built the adjoining section, and Zakkur son of Imri built next to them."

Nehemiah 3:8, "Uzziel son of Harhaiah, one of the goldsmiths, repaired the next section; and Hananiah, one of the perfume-makers, made repairs next to that. They restored Jerusalem as far as the Broad Wall."

Nehemiah 3:22, "The repairs next to him were made by the priests from the surrounding region."

As we continue reading Nehemiah 3, we also see people who rebuilt the wall where there seemed to be no personal benefit to them. One example is the people of Jericho. Jericho was a long way from Jerusalem, and if it was ever attacked, the walls around Jerusalem were not going to do the people of Jericho any good. They had their own wall to worry about, and yet they came to pursue a greater good. After all, having strong walls around Jerusalem was good for all the people of Israel, because God had made it clear that Jerusalem was the City of David and the place that His glory was going to dwell in the temple. The people of Jericho were willing to invest their own "sweat equity" in order to serve Israel. The same could be said of the priests from the surrounding region in verse 22. They saw that in some sense, as goes Jerusalem, so goes the nation.

But there are others we see serving for the benefit of others in this passage. Did you notice there were several different people who were serving out of their area of specialty and gifting? People from all kinds of vocations coming together to build the wall. We see merchants, goldsmiths, perfumers, priests, and guards all serving outside of their vocations. They all became wall builders for a season, and they did not receive a salary or directly benefit from the enterprise. They did it out of a desire to serve the larger community, and the time they invested in wall building meant that they lost time investing in their own trade. Even Nehemiah himself was not a wall builder by profession. His vocation was being a cupbearer to the king, but he set aside his day job for a season to become a wall builder for the kingdom.

When we read through this chapter, it should inspire us to serve for a larger kingdom purpose, and it might be doing something that has nothing to do with your vocation and does not serve any sort of vested interest of yours. The New Testament is clear that the primary place we are commanded to serve is in the church. There are many other causes to support and non-profits to partner with, but God has given us spiritual gifts that we are to first use in serving in the church. There may be a big difference between your vocation, what you do Monday through Friday, and your place of service in the church. Your vocation is what you do for a living to provide for your family, what you get paid to do. We must be faithful to these vocations, while also recognizing that there is a larger kingdom, we are a part of and need to contribute to.

It is amazing when you look around the church and see many people serving where they do not necessarily have a vested interest; they are serving because they desire to benefit others. I can think back over my years at Cottonwood Creek Church where I have seen people serving in the Children's or Student Ministry who do not have any kids in the church. They are serving where they do not have any vested interest, but their service is vital to the kingdom of God. It is a beautiful thing that brings much honor to Christ. As you are seeking to find your place within the church, listen to the Spirit's leading, and do not discount the possibility that God may be calling you to serve Him in a place where you don't have a vested interest. It is very likely to be in an area where this is a great need, like the need to rebuild Jerusalem's wall so many years ago.

4. Some Worked Double-Duty

Nehemiah 3:5, "The next section was repaired by the men of Tekoa, but their nobles would not put their shoulders to the work under their supervisors..."

Nehemiah 3:27, "Next to them, the men of Tekoa repaired another section, from the great projecting tower to the wall of Ophel."

There have always been those who seem to go above and beyond in building the kingdom of God. You know, the people who always seem like they are involved everywhere and with everything. One prominent example of this is found in our passage here, and it is one you must do a little digging to find. If you notice, verses 5 and 27 mention "the men of Tekoa," who apparently are doing double duty by building two different sections of the wall. Notice that these men are from another area. Tekoa was a small town five miles south of Bethlehem, the home of the prophet Amos (Amos 1:1). These men came from a good distance to contribute to the greater good of Jerusalem and the Israelite people, and they made twice the effort in doing so!

But there is more. You see, there is only one sour note in this entire chapter, and it comes in verse 5 where we are told that the nobles of the Tekoites "would not put their shoulders to the work under their supervisors." This is a notable exception to the rule of everyone serving and finding their place, evidence that not every Judean participated in the rebuilding of the wall (as it seems they should have). Not everyone was enthusiastic about the rebuilding. These Tekoite nobles did not cooperate in building the city's defenses, perhaps thinking that such "nitty-gritty" work was below them. But then an amazing thing happened. The men of Tekoa made up for their nobles' shameful refusal to participate. They pulled double duty not only by building two segments of the wall, but by filling in for another segment of Israel that should have been participating. I wish I could shake their hand today and say: "Now that's how it's done!"

But this is how it often is in God's kingdom. There is a common observation in the church that 20% of the people do 80% of the work. That is a sad observation to the extent it is true. It has been said that "hard work spotlights the character of people; some turn up their sleeves, some turn up their noses, and some don't turn up at all." It is a wonderful thing that we have folks in our churches that are willing to pull double duty, but it should not be necessary for them to do so because God's design is that *everyone* serves in the church.

In fact, it is for our spiritual good that we serve in the church. To see this, think about the two major bodies of water in Israel: The Sea of Galilee and the Dead Sea. The Sea of Galilee is fed by the Jordan River and several underground springs, and it is vibrant and fresh, teeming with fish and life-giving in every way. But the Dead Sea is the very opposite of the Sea of Galilee. It is, by its very name, "Dead." But why? I submit to you that one of the reasons that it is dead is that water flows in (from the Jordan River) but never flows out. It receives but never gives. And so, it is with us. If we do not serve and give, then we become like the Dead Sea. Yes, as God's Children, we need to receive from others---through the teaching of God's Word, through others serving us in tangible ways. In order for us to flourish, we need to serve and give back in ways that serve others. It seems to me that too many people in our churches are more like the Dead Sea than the Sea of Galilee, receiving sermons, gifts, and service from others but never giving back. All inflow, no outflow. When this happens, we no longer become useful to God or His church—so make a commitment now to start serving and giving back to your church.

5. *Some Did the Dirty Work*

Nehemiah 3:14, "The Dung Gate was repaired by Malkijah son of Rekab, ruler of the district of Beth Hakkerem. He rebuilt it and put its doors with their bolts and bars in place."

When we look at the names of the gates built around the wall of Jerusalem, some of them seem exciting and inspiring. Names like "Sheep Gate," "Fish Gate," "Horse Gate" and "Water Gate" seem like places everyone would want to serve. After all, who does not like sheep, fish, horses, and water! These gates also played a vital role in the industry of Jerusalem necessary for people to live there. Rebuilding the Fish Gate is what allowed fish from the Mediterranean Sea and from the Sea of Galilee to be brought into the fish market where people could purchase them for their nutrition (and culinary delight!). This might seem like a high-profile job that you could brag about the rest of your life.

However, you probably noticed one specific gate as you were reading through this chapter that would likely *not* be the gate everyone was lining up to rebuild, and that was--the Dung Gate. As you may have guessed, there is nothing, and I mean nothing, that was glamorous or exciting about rebuilding the Dung Gate. It was the gate that all the trash, refuse and, yes, even the dung, was taken out of to the Valley of Hinnom—the trash dump just outside the city. That sounds like dirty work to me! However, even though it was dirty work, it was vitally important work for keeping the city healthy and clean. We do not know anything about Malkijah other than he was the one who stepped up to do this important work. The Lord raised him up to do the dirty work, and everyone in the city benefitted from it.

We need to pause here and recognize that in the Kingdom of God there is great significance in the trivial and even dirty work that we may be called to do. Rebuilding the wall of Jerusalem was an exciting task, but in order for it to be completed in the way that was necessary it required some not so glamourous work. The same is true in the church today. It may not be glamorous to clean toilets or wash dishes or vacuum the carpet or clean the nursery after a kid with stomach issues has come through, but these things matter greatly in the eyes of God. Not everyone will step up to do the dirty work, but those who recognize these as opportunities to follow Jesus when He said, "whoever wants to become great among you must be your servant" (Matthew 20:26) will take them up knowing they are following their Master, the One Who did the dirtiest, least-glamourous work we could ever imagine: dying a horrific death on the cross for the sake of others.

There is indeed significance in the trivial. Sir Arthur Conan Doyle was right when he said, "the little things are infinitely the most important." If you are wondering how you might serve the church, may I encourage you to consider doing the dirty work? And can I encourage you to consider doing it with passion, knowing that you are serving in a way that is vital in the Kingdom? It is often thankless work, and as we have said, there is not much glamor in it. But we know it is work that pleases our heavenly Father and that we will be richly rewarded for one day.

Next Steps

We have seen how Nehemiah chapter 3 offers us a picture of God's people serving in the Kingdom by finding their place. We have said that everyone has a place. That was true in the Old Covenant, and it is even more true in the New Covenant. Consider a passage like Ephesians 4:11-12, 16 which says, "So Christ himself gave the apostles, the prophets, the evangelists, the pastors and teachers, to equip his people for works of service, so that the body of Christ may be built up... From him the whole body, joined and held together by every supporting ligament, grows and builds itself up in love, as each part does its work." Here we see that Paul understands the church as a body where every part plays a role. Just like in Nehemiah's day, there are leadership roles, such as pastors who are called to teach and equip God's people for "works of service." But I hope you see that they are just one part of the body. They only play a very particular role. The vision is that *everyone* has a place to serve in their local church, with the end result being that the "body of Christ is built up."

He even mentions supporting ligaments. Several years ago, I tore my bicep tendon off the bone. While the pain of that trauma was great, the bigger question was how I was going to reattach it? Truthfully, I did not have to reattach it. I have other muscles in my arm that could have compensated. I even had another arm that had a fully functioning bicep. I could have survived without reattaching the bicep. But I would have never functioned at my highest capacity had I not reattached the ligament and done the physical therapy required to strengthen and heal that muscle. My body would not have been as strong without that one supporting ligament. The supporting, serving role that it must play, while easy to overlook, is vital to my entire body working as it should.

And so, we return to the question: do you know your place? Do you know what role God has created you to play within the body? Do you have an outlet to be able to serve, to join in the larger kingdom effort, as these Israelites did under Nehemiah so many years ago? We know that we do not serve God or the church to earn our salvation; Ephesians 2:8-10 clearly teaches that "it is by grace you have been saved, through faith..." He has it all lined up; we just need to step up to the plate and say with the prophet Isaiah: "Here I am Lord; send me!"

If each of us can find our place of serving in the church, watch out! Just like the miracle of rebuilding the wall took place in *52 days* in Nehemiah's day—God can do similar miracles, and even greater, among us, all for our good and His glory. So, are you in a group, serving in a place where you have a vested interest or serving somewhere simply for the benefit of others? Are you serving in a way that goes the extra mile? Are you doing the dirty work so God's kingdom can flourish? All of these are blessed and high callings. Your local church will never function at its full capacity without your gifting, and you will never be as strong spiritually as you could be, if you are not finding that arena of service. Here are four questions to help guide you in taking that next step toward serving in the place that God has for you.

1. Are you connected to a church and ready to start rebuilding?

1 Corinthians 12:12-14, "Just as a body, though one, has many parts, but all its many parts form one body, so it is with Christ. For we were all baptized by one Spirit so as to form one body—whether Jews or Gentiles, slave or free—and we were all given the one Spirit to drink. Even so the body is not made up of one part but of many."

2. Are you in a group, ready to join a group, or willing to start a group?

Hebrews 10:23-25, "Let us hold unswervingly to the hope we profess, for he who promised is faithful. And let us consider how we may spur one another on toward love and good deeds, not giving up meeting together, as some are in the habit of doing, but encouraging one another—and all the more as you see the Day approaching."

3. Are you ready to start using your talents, skills, and abilities to serve God and others?

Romans 12:11, "Never be lacking in zeal, but keep your spiritual fervor, serving the Lord."

4. Have you taken a spiritual gifts survey to see where you might best fit in serving?

1 Corinthians 12:4-7, "There are different kinds of gifts, but the same Spirit distributes them. There are different kinds of service, but the same Lord. There are different kinds of working, but in all of them and in everyone it is the same God at work. Now to each one the manifestation of the Spirit is given for the common good."

Prayer: Heavenly Father, it is amazing what You accomplish through Your people. I am in awe as I look at how You used Nehemiah and all the various groups of Israelites to rebuild the wall of Jerusalem. I want to see You do amazing things in our day. And so, would You continue to guide me into the good works You have already prepared for me? Would You prompt my heart by Your Holy Spirit to find my place of service within the church? And would You continue to keep my eyes fixed on Jesus, Who went before us in being the servant Who served for the benefit of others, did double duty, and took on the dirty work of dealing with my sin on the cross? May I become a servant after His heart by your grace. In Christ's name I pray...Amen.

Chapter 3: Keep the Mission

Read Nehemiah 5:1-19

Big Picture

How do we rebuild a life that matters? By keeping the mission which God has given to the church. As we will see, there are many obstacles to doing so. In this chapter, we are going to consider the *internal* obstacles to keeping this mission, focusing on how conflict within the "house of faith" can distract us from doing what the Lord desires us to do and being who He desires us to be. In the next chapter, we will focus on *external* obstacles, those outside the church who would seek to deter us from our mission. Being able to deal with both of these obstacles is key to rebuilding a life that matters and getting our life to better align with God's mission for us.

The Call to Unity: Our Being One in Christ

Galatians 3:28 makes one thing abundantly clear: even though the church is made up of different genders, different races, different classes, "we are all one in Christ Jesus." That is the reality which Christ brought about by reconciling all of us to God and to one another by His work on the cross. There is a unity which marks us as a people that no one can destroy. And yet, in Ephesians 4:3, Paul writes this: "Make every effort to keep the unity of the Spirit through the bond of peace." Why does Paul have to exhort the church to make every effort to keep the unity that we already have by the Spirit? Because the fact is, even though we are united in Christ, we often act as if we don't and allow other distinctions to cause *disunity* among us. Welcome to the real world!

Through the first four chapters of Nehemiah, we have seen that Nehemiah was given the call to rebuild Jerusalem's wall, that he developed the plan, that he spent time in prayer, that he cast the vision, that he acquired the necessary resources, and that he united the people in the incredible rebuilding effort. There was opposition (we'll get to that more in the next chapter), but perhaps most disappointing was what we read about in chapter 5. It is here we are told about the internal divisions and tensions that existed among God's people as they were called to this kingdom work of rebuilding the wall. These tensions inevitably led to conflict and even confrontation which detracted from the very work they have been called to do. The only way the rebuilding effort was going to be successful, the only way they were going to keep to their mission, is if this conflict was dealt with in a way that was effective and wise.

Nehemiah 5 thus presents us with a passage that gives us great guidance on how to handle conflict in our lives and in the church. Paul exhorts us to make every effort to keep the unity that is ours in Christ. Such unity is vitally important if the church is going to be as effective in keeping our mission, fulfilling the Great Commission. In fact, Jesus says that our unity is a key factor in whether the world will look at the church and believe the Gospel (John 17:20-21). Far too often churches don't accomplish all they could because of conflict and a resulting lack of unity.

The Need to Call for Unity: Fleshly Conflict

But *why* is there conflict among believers? What is the reason that we must try to maintain unity? If we have the Spirit of God in common, and that same Spirit would never be in conflict with Himself, then why is this so difficult? Why is it that when we look out at churches today sometimes, we see nothing *but* conflict and a lack of unity? The answer is actually quite simple: it is called the "flesh." Every follower of Christ knows that they are one in Christ with every other Christian; every follower of Christ knows that they are called on mission with others to fulfill the Great Commission and that unity is central to accomplishing that mission. But every Christ follower is still battling "the flesh," a biblical term used to refer to our sin nature that we still struggle with all the way to glory. In our flesh, we desire to be proved right rather than die to our rights. In our flesh, we hold a fellow Christian in very low regard. In our flesh, we think *we* know how to accomplish something and that *someone else* doesn't. The result of this fleshly battle is discord, difficulty, distraction, and disunity.

In Nehemiah's day, the Israelites knew that they were one people, united by God's covenantal purpose, and that they had a mission to rebuild the wall. In fact, they had longed for decades to rebuild the wall, and now the work had started! These were exciting times. But then, the problems arise. Satan would love nothing more than to throw a wrench into this show of unity before the watching world. Nehemiah 5 shows us the specifics, which involved an economic crisis and class divisions that threatened the entire mission. Let us look and see what we can learn from this chapter about how to successfully navigate conflict in the church as it arises so that we will be able to keep the mission. We're going to see four realities of these internal conflicts and think about how being aware of each of them helps us prepare for such conflicts not if, but when, they come.

1. Be Ready: We Will Encounter Conflict

Nehemiah 5:1-6, "Now the men and their wives raised a great outcry against their fellow Jews. Some were saying, "We and our sons and daughters are numerous; in order for us to eat and stay alive, we must get grain." Others were saying, "We are mortgaging our fields, our vineyards and our homes to get grain during the famine." Still others were saying, "We have had to borrow money to pay the king's tax on our fields and vineyards. Although we are of the same flesh and blood as our fellow Jews and though our children are as good as theirs, yet we have to subject our sons and daughters to slavery. Some of our daughters have already been enslaved, but we are powerless, because our fields and our vineyards belong to others."

The "great outcry" from the people literally stopped the work on the wall and threatened the success of rebuilding it. The specific problem here is an economic problem: the folks who have been engaged in the work of rebuilding are now at a financial breaking point. We see that specifically they are experiencing a lack of adequate food (vs. 2), the need to mortgage their fields to find short term cash to buy grain, perhaps even losing their fields altogether (vs. 3), the strain of having to borrow money to pay exorbitant taxes (vs. 4), and even the cruel situation of having to sell family members into indentured servitude to pay off debts (vs. 5). This was not a good situation and one ready to cultivate internal strife among God's people. But it is particularly rife with conflict because it exposed a source of division among them: rich Jews had enough stored up to feed themselves, while the poor were pressed to give up family members as collateral for debts just to survive. In pursuit of the accepted mission, difficulties had arisen much more for the poor than the rich. For the work of rebuilding to be effective and strong, the people needed to stay focused on their mission, but that is hard to do when the basic necessities of life aren't being provided for.

Here we can note that people are often disillusioned in the church when there is strife or conflict. Of course, these things are always troublesome and should be addressed as soon and effectively as possible, but we must remember that people inside the church are still people—broken people working alongside other broken people for the Kingdom of God. In this sense, we need to recognize that in this fallen world conflict, of one sort or another, is inevitable. This doesn't excuse it; it rather prepares us appropriately to be ready to deal with it. It is not a matter of if, but when, it will come. Thus, a key to being involved in God's work is not to think that it will be marked by the absence of conflict, but rather to understand that it will happen and to be able to work through that conflict in a biblical manner when it does. Jesus said, "where two or three gather in my name, there I am with them" (Matthew 18:20). But I have also found that where two or three gather, even when that gathering is in Christ's name, there will also be conflict. Every family, office, organization, and friend group will have conflict at some point. It is the same for the church—regardless of how great or successful the church.

In particular here we see one form of conflict that often arises, and that is conflict around issues of money. This passage reminds us that money problems among God's people is nothing new. This is why the New Testament provides so much teaching around this. Jesus warns that "you cannot serve both God and money" (Matthew 6:24); Paul exhorts the rich among them "to do good, to be rich in good deeds, and to be generous and willing to share" (1 Timothy 6:18). It is particularly important to see that the New Testament continues to emphasize (as the Old Testament did) that those who have been blessed with riches have an obligation to look out for their poorer brothers and sisters in Christ. The financial divisions which exist among us can be one of the greatest hindrances to our unity in Christ. We must see that caring for the poor and vulnerable among us is one of the most distinctive aspects of the Christian community and allows us to better fulfill the mission: instead of strife and division there can be love and unity!

2. Be Wise: Conflicts Should Be Handled Carefully

Nehemiah 5:6-9, 11-13, "When I heard their outcry and these charges, I was very angry. I pondered them in my mind and then accused the nobles and officials. I told them, "You are charging your own people interest!" So I called together a large meeting to deal with them and said: "As far as possible, we have bought back our fellow Jews who were sold to the Gentiles. Now you are selling your own people, only for them to be sold back to us!" They kept quiet, because they could find nothing to say. So I continued, "What you are doing is not right. Shouldn't you walk in the fear of our God to avoid the reproach of our Gentile enemies?"... Give back to them immediately their fields, vineyards, olive groves and houses, and also the interest you are charging them—one percent of the money, grain, new wine and olive oil." "We will give it back," they said. "And we will not demand anything more from them. We will do as you say." Then I summoned the priests and made the nobles and officials take an oath to do what they had promised. I also shook out the folds of my robe and said, "In this way may God shake out of their house and possessions anyone who does not keep this promise. So may such a person be shaken out and emptied!" At this the whole assembly said, "Amen," and praised the Lord. And the people did as they had promised."

With any problem or conflict, there is a right way and a wrong way to handle it. I have seen some small conflicts made larger because of the way they were poorly handled. I have also seen very large conflicts quickly diffused because of the biblical way in which they were handled. The key is developing wisdom based on biblical teaching as we step into these conflicts, being careful that we address the issue in a way that cares for those involved, handles the sin issue at play, and seeks to honor Christ by looking to Him to be the One Who brings about reconciliation and a change in heart and behavior as it is necessary.

Now we might ask at this point: are we willing to risk derailing the mission in order to glorify God and care for the brethren when there is conflict? This is essentially what Nehemiah risked when he confronted the wealthy Jews on behalf of those of whom they had taken advantage. To confront the people who had the wealth and power was a risky move, because if they withdrew their support it is likely the whole building project would fail. But Nehemiah recognizes that the building project will fail if he *does not* address the conflict. The poorer of the Israelites that were doing so much to contribute were out of money, and without seeing a way forward, they would be done. The wall was being built at a spectacular rate, but that was going to come to a crashing halt if something didn't change. Nehemiah had to take the risk. He had to face this problem, and he knew he needed to do it carefully.

Now, when we face problems, we always need wisdom to know not only how best to handle it, but even whether we need to handle it. We know we can't stop doing everything to fix every problem we see or confront every wrong doer we come across... we'd never make it home for dinner at night! We do need to think about whether we are the person to take on the problem, and we need to consider whether we have the resources to take on the problem. But we must never let this careful consideration prevent us from confronting the problem when we are called upon to do so.

Nehemiah's wise response to this conflict offers us several solid principles for resolving conflicts well when we are called to. Let's examine four of those principles here:

1. After Anger, Exercise Self-Control: Anger is a God-given emotion than can bring God glory; Jesus was angry with the moneychangers at the temple who were turning a holy endeavor of temple sacrifices into a money-making enterprise. However, we need to exercise self-control amidst this anger, or else we can make matters worse instead of making them better. We see here that Nehemiah was "very angry" (vs. 6). Upon hearing the complaints of the poorer classes concerning the richer ones, Nehemiah is outraged. Everything that the wealthier Jews were doing in their relations with their less fortunate brethren was unacceptable. Had he acted out of rage, Nehemiah probably would have done more harm than good. Nehemiah didn't go off in a rage; rather, he stopped and cooled off. That is significant! Verse 7 tells us that Nehemiah pondered theses things in his mind before acting. He considered the matter deeply and thoughtfully (and probably prayerfully). He examined the problem from all sides, searching for the best way to handle the situation. He also developed a plan that would help him to channel his righteous anger. So, before you act in an aggressive and detrimental anger, take your cue from

Nehemiah: regain your composure and develop a plan. This will help you from either reacting too softly or overreacting, which in both cases is likely to prevent there being any real changes.

2. Attack the Problem, Not the Person: Nehemiah recognized that they were all "on the same team." To view the rich in this situation as the enemy that needed to be subdued would have made the matter worse. Instead, Nehemiah draws on the backdrop of his knowledge of Scripture to address the problem manifesting among God's people: they are not being faithful to the Law where it called for them to care for the poor among them and not charge them exorbitant interest. This is expressed by Nehemiah when he says: "what you are doing is not right." He didn't say: "You are not right;" he said that what they were doing was not in alignment with God's will for them, and then he began to make his case. Nehemiah was singling out the wrong actions and not the wrong people. It is always easier to settle the problem if we frame things as all of us trying to solve a problem, rather than point a finger at the problem people.

3. Speak Privately Before Acting Publically: Notice that Nehemiah did not take this public prematurely. After he had cooled off and developed his plan, he went to those he perceived to be at the heart of the problem and spoke with them personally and privately. No doubt he used some pretty blunt language in that meeting, but since it was a private meeting this did not create an issue or highjack the resolution of the conflict. If these same accusations were made in a public setting, it would have been that much harder for these rich Israelites to acknowledge the error of their ways; that is just human nature. Nehemiah was wise to go to them privately first, rather than begin with a public confrontation, which could quickly introduce the elements of pride or embarrassment. Ultimately, we have little chance of success when we don't show respect to those we believe are in the wrong by going to them first.

4. Act Publically When Necessary: Nehemiah won over the rich Israelites at his private meeting (vs. 12), but he felt that since the nature of the offense had been public, there now needed to be a public declaration of their new intent. Nehemiah didn't just want the wealthy Jews to *privately* promise to return—without conditions—any land seized due to unpaid debts along with any interest collected (vs. 11); he knew that such a promise needed to be proclaimed *publically* so that the problem would be addressed more immediately and so there would be greater accountability for the wealthy Jews in following up on their promise. This public proclamation would have *immediately* relieved the stress that these poor families had been facing, and there was not a minute to spare in getting the rebuilding effort complete. It was vital that the divisions within the community caused by mistreatment of certain classes by others were immediately addressed and put to rest. Fortunately, for everyone involved, the wealthy Jews listened and did what he commanded (vs. 12–13).

There are two things we can take away from this section of the passage that emerge from the principles above. The first is that while we need wisdom to determine which problems to ignore and which ones to confront, we also need courage to take on the problems that we decide to take on. Nehemiah was not asking "what would be popular here?" he was asking "how do I need to be faithful here?" Too often, leaders ask the first question when they should be asking the second. Nehemiah cares about doing what was right regardless of the personal cost to him. We need more leaders who embrace this sort of mentality. Dietrich Bonhoeffer has said, "Nothing can be more cruel than the leniency which abandons others to their sin. Nothing can be more compassionate than the severe reprimand which calls another Christian in one's community back from the path of sin." By confronting the wealthy Jews so strongly, he risked the loss of participation and support of these Jews in the rebuilding of the wall; nevertheless, Nehemiah understood that the wall was secondary to the unity of the community and exercises the courage necessary to call them out. If the poorer Jews were allowed to be mistreated, then God would not bless the mission. In this way, standing up for the weak and vulnerable at the expense of the mission is itself the only sure way of keeping the mission. Whatever God blesses, He will ensure its success; alternatively, whatever God refuses to bless will not bring any worthwhile success. When conflict arises, faithful Christians must address any wrongdoing comprehensively and courageously. Christians must confront anyone and everyone who mistreats other community members because ultimately the community mission is at stake.

The second thing we need to see is that Jesus provides us particular guidance on how to confront others about a wrong. Jesus said in Matthew 18:15-17 "If your brother or sister sins, go and point out their fault, just between the two of you. If they listen to you, you have won them over. But if they will not listen, take one or two others along, so that 'every matter may be established by the testimony of two or three witnesses.' If they still refuse to listen, tell it to the church; and if they refuse to listen even to the church, treat them as you would a pagan or a tax collector." Do you see that what Nehemiah demonstrated aligns with what Jesus presents here? He first went to them personally and privately, spelling out the problem and not being afraid to identify the sin. He won them over, so the public gathering was one of confirming the next steps rather than a public proclamation of unrepentant sin. Today we see too many people confronting others in a way that does not follow the biblical model. One only needs to think about the number of public attacks that are made on social media

alone to see that this is true. We are called to go to the brother
or sister privately first, and if they do not hear us the next step is
to bring along two or three witnesses to help get their attention.
We need to follow Nehemiah's example and Jesus' teaching when
dealing with conflict and sin within the church.

3. Be Out Front: Leaders Set the Example

Nehemiah 5:10, "I and my brothers and my men are also lend-ing the people money and grain. But let us stop charging interest!"

*Nehemiah 5:14-15, 17-18, "Moreover, from the twentieth year
of King Artaxerxes, when I was appointed to be their governor in the
land of Judah, until his thirty-second year—twelve years—neither I
nor my brothers ate the food allotted to the governor. But the earlier
governors—those preceding me—placed a heavy burden on the people
and took forty shekels of silver from them in addition to food and wine.
Their assistants also lorded it over the people. But out of reverence for
God I did not act like that....Furthermore, a hundred and fifty Jews
and officials ate at my table, as well as those who came to us from the
surrounding nations. Each day one ox, six choice sheep and some poul-try were prepared for me, and every ten days an abundant supply of
wine of all kinds. In spite of all this, I never demanded the food allotted
to the governor, because the demands were heavy on these people."*

As a leader, Nehemiah understood the value of setting a
good example for others. If we are going to stay on mission for
God, character matters. How we live out our faith matters much
more than the words we proclaim about our faith, especially if we
are leaders in the effort.

Notice first that Nehemiah exhibited great humility as a
leader here. He was willing to acknowledge that as a wealthier

Jew he was also involved in the lending practices that were becoming so oppressive of the poorer Jews. He doesn't deny that he has also been acting in a way that may not be in full alignment with God's law; rather he takes this opportunity to recognize this and express his willingness to change. Far too often we are quick to point out someone else's faults without being honest enough to acknowledge our own. In Nehemiah's case, he admitted that he and his brothers were also charging interest in a way that made him implicated. This was even part of what likely got him buy-in with the other wealthier folks: he was at the first of the line to both acknowledge his fault and also repent of that behavior. That sent shock waves through the assembly! If their leader was willing to recognize his fault and immediately change course, then they could too.

But the passage goes on to describe another important way that Nehemiah led by example: he made personal sacrifices for the purpose of pleasing God and serving God's people. As governor of Judah, Nehemiah had significant economic privileges that he could draw on as desired by taxing the people. As one Bible scholar explained "a Persian governor had the right to collect taxes from his subjects for his own treasury, not just for the Crown. Monies collected in this way paid for local projects and supported the administration. Food and drink went to the governor and his household."[5] However, it seems that Nehemiah was willing to sacrifice all of this for the good of his Jewish brethren. Indeed, "Bigger to him than his prestige as governor, better to him than the privileges the governor would enjoy, was the good that would come to the people as the kingdom of God was advanced through the building of the walls. Nehemiah wanted God's name exalted and God's weak and vulnerable people protected."[6] Amidst all of the duties

---

5   Walton, et al. *IVP Bible Background Commentary*, 476.

6   Hamilton, Jr., *Exalting Jesus in Nehemiah*, 131.

that he had as governor of this region (including hosting foreign diplomats), it seems that he paid for these expenses out of his own pocket rather than tax the (already over-taxed) Israelites. Thus, he led the mission of rebuilding from the front and by example.

We can take two things away from this section. First, we must be warned that not everyone who serves God and leads God's people provide the example that they should. We can all think of people who say they are committed Christ followers, but their lives don't reflect that of someone who lives well for the faith. This is even more tragic when this person is in a leadership role, but that is the reality. Nehemiah himself acknowledges here that those who came before him did not exhibit the godly characters of good leaders (vs. 15). There have been times in my ministry that people have come to me and told me about being hurt by a pastor, deacon, or other Christian leader in the church. Sadly, it happens more than we care to admit. However, we can't let that keep us from accomplishing the mission that God has set before each of us. In the New Testament, Peter gave a clear example of the lifestyle that leaders in the church need to exhibit. 1 Peter 5:1-4 says, "To the elders among you, I appeal as a fellow elder and a witness of Christ's sufferings who also will share in the glory to be revealed: Be shepherds of God's flock that is under your care, watching over them—not because you must, but because you are willing, as God wants you to be; not pursuing dishonest gain, but eager to serve; not lording it over those entrusted to you, but being examples to the flock. And when the Chief Shepherd appears, you will receive the crown of glory that will never fade away." We see that this is the sort of character exhibited by Nehemiah, and it is the sort of character we should be looking for in our Christian leaders today.

Another example of this sort of integrity from a Christian leader is the apostle Paul. Aside from the Lord Himself, Paul was one of the greatest examples of sacrificial service in the New Testament. Paul knew his mission and frequently sacrificed privileges for the purposes of spreading the Gospel and caring for those to whom he ministered. For example, in 2 Thessalonians 3:6-9 Paul wrote, "Now we command you, brethren, in the name of our Lord Jesus Christ, that you keep away from every brother who leads an unruly life and not according to the tradition which you received from us. For you yourselves know how you ought to follow our example, because we did not act in an undisciplined manner among you, nor did we eat anyone's bread without paying for it, but with labor and hardship we kept working night and day so that we would not be a burden to any of you; not because we do not have the right to this, but in order to offer ourselves as a model for you, so that you would follow our example." Like Nehemiah, Paul sacrificed personally for the mission to advance. Christian leaders today must act likewise in self-sacrificial service to those whom God has placed under their care, in order to be an example of love and concern. This is the only true way to keep the Christian mission. As Harry Ironside once said, "No sacrifice should be too great for Him Who gave Himself for us."

But the second thing we should take away from this section is the call that we see for leaders to lead by example not just in sacrifice, but also in repentance. Nehemiah did not lie or try to hide behind a false veneer; he openly recognized where his life was not fully aligned with God's Word and sought to make that change immediately in his life. Being honest about our failures is one of the most important ways for leaders to lead. To be willing to confess a fault, ask for forgiveness, and to then change your way can be a powerful thing for your followers to behold. It reminds them that no one, apart from Christ, is perfect. We are all stumbling our way into the Kingdom by God's grace, and in the mission God has given the church it is vitally important for the leaders to remember, especially if they are being successful, that they too need the work of Christ on their behalf, and they too have much room to grow in godliness.

4. Be Single-Minded: Conflict Doesn't Have to Derail the Mission

Nehemiah 5:16, "Instead, I devoted myself to the work on this wall. All my men were assembled there for the work; we did not acquire any land."

Nehemiah 5:19, "Remember me with favor, my God, for all I have done for these people."

The mission of Nehemiah and the children of Israel was to rebuild the wall. Because of Nehemiah's wisdom and sacrifice, the mission was not derailed by severe and seemingly irreparable divisions. Nehemiah realized that if the mission was going to be accomplished, he had to make sure that *all* of God's people, including the poor ones, could be a part of seeing it complete. To operate as effectively as we can for the Kingdom of God we need to deal with conflict as quickly as possible and get back on mission. Not every conflict needs to stop progress or even the work ahead. Not every conflict has an easy or simple solution. However, some conflict must be dealt with in order for the people of God to complete the work of God. A single-mindedness of vision will help us recognize what is hindering the mission and therefore what we need to address in order for that mission to be accomplished.

We must not forget that God's heart is for His people, and that His mission concerns them as well. Nehemiah was not building Jerusalem's walls merely to protect the city, and certainly not to protect God. Nehemiah put all of his efforts into rebuilding the walls in order to protect God's people and bring them security and rest. Nehemiah was willing to sacrifice his own comfort and privileges in order to care for God's people and accomplish his mission. He saw the bigger picture that enabled him to stay focus, make sacrifices, and courageously step toward conflict because he saw how that conflict threatened the mission.

For us, we see Jesus as the ultimate example of a leader who had a single-mindedness for the mission. Matthew 9:35-38 tells us that, "Jesus went through all the towns and villages, teaching in their synagogues, proclaiming the good news of the kingdom and healing every disease and sickness. When He saw the crowds, He had compassion on them, because they were harassed and helpless, like sheep without a shepherd. Then He said to His disciples, "The harvest is plentiful but the workers are few. Ask the Lord of the harvest, therefore, to send out workers into His harvest field." Notice that Jesus is both caring for the people that He encounters, while calling His disciples to recognize the larger mission. Jesus encountered many conflicts in His ministry; in fact, nearly every encounter He had with the religious leaders was a conflict! He also addressed many a conflict among His disciples, whether it be an argument about who was the greatest in the Kingdom (what a silly argument!) or whether there was time for children to come and see Him (of course there was!). Jesus understood that conflict prevents us from focusing on the mission in the way we should, and yet conflict can become an opportunity for us to grow in becoming more equipped for the mission. Thanks to Jesus' faithfulness to His mission (coming to seek and save the lost by laying down His life for us!), we have been given everything we need in order to accomplish the mission which God has given the church!

So, as you seek to follow Christ in your life—remember the Mission. If we aren't careful, we can actually forget what the mission of every believer is. Our mission isn't about voting, getting rich, or getting our dream job. Our mission is about bringing others to faith in Christ. In Matthew 28:18-20, Jesus made this abundantly clear: "Then Jesus came to them and said, "All authority in heaven and on earth has been given to me. Therefore go and make disciples of all nations, baptizing them in the name of the Father and of the Son and of the Holy Spirit, and teaching them to obey everything I have commanded you. And surely I am with you always, to the very end of the age." This is a mission worth making every sacrifice for, and worth wisely and courageously dealing with every conflict which we come across. And when we remember that the heart of God's mission involves loving others, then we can understand that whatever materialistic advantages we may gain in this life are irrelevant in the larger scheme of the Christian life, we will be able to better align with God's mission, asking how we can better keep the mission by sacrificing for the good of others and the glory of God.

Next Steps:

This would be a good time to pause, like Nehemiah did, and ponder: What is your mission? Everyone has some sort of mission in life that they are living for, even if that mission is getting through life with as much happiness and as little pain and difficulty as possible. Yet, for Christians, life is so much more that the overly simplistic equation of "more happiness and less pain equal a fulfilled life." A suffering Christian who lives out his mission faithfully for Christ lives a life infinitely more fulfilling than an unbeliever who gains all physical and mental happiness while avoiding all pain. As Jesus pondered in Matthew 16:26, "For what will it profit a man if he gains the whole world and forfeits his soul?"

So, how does your life align with the mission God has given the church? Have conflicts which have occurred in the church perhaps soured you and prevented you from taking the next steps on that mission? Have you found it difficult to make some of the necessary sacrifices to follow Christ on His mission of taking up your cross and dying to yourself for the sake of others? If so, look anew to God for help to refocus on the mission and keep to it no matter what trials and tribulations may come. In the Gospel, we have a supernatural mission that seeks the ultimate well-being of all of God's people forever. This will sometimes conflict with our own personal missions, causing us to choose one over the other; yet God promises that fidelity to His mission will not disappoint but will lead to rewards and blessings that last into eternity.

Prayer: Lord, help me to trust You that the life You have called me to live and the mission You have set before me is the most fulfilling path. May I take great encouragement from the example of leaders such as Nehemiah who led by example and dealt with conflict within the people of God so effectively. May You be pleased to raise up more people like Nehemiah in my day, and may I be in that number, for the accomplishment of the mission You have given the church, and for Your greater glory. In Jesus' name I pray...amen.

Chapter 4: Face Your Opposition

Read Nehemiah 4:1-23 & 6:1-19

Big Picture

How do we rebuild a life that matters? By facing the opposition which inevitably comes as we seek to fulfill the mission which God has given the church. In the last chapter we considered the *internal* obstacles to keeping this mission; now we will focus on *external* obstacles, those outside the church who would seek to deter us from our mission. Being able to deal with both obstacles is key to rebuilding a life that matters and getting our life to better align with God's mission for us.

Opposition is Inevitable

The people of God have always faced opposition. It has come in the form of murderous enemies and the inclinations of our sin natures. The Israelites faced opposition from Pharaoh while they were in captivity in Egypt and from their own rebellious hearts when they were wandering in the desert. Even when the Israelites made it into the Promised Land, they faced opposition from both the Philistines and from false prophets leading the people into idolatry. Later in the Old Testament we encounter the crippling opposition of unfaithful kings and destructive empires like that of the Assyrians or Babylonians.

In the New Testament, Jesus tells His followers to assume that they will have trouble (John 16:33) and will be hated as He Himself was hated (Matthew 5:11). Paul assumes that the realities of trouble, hardship, persecution, famine, nakedness, danger, and sword will accompany the Christian life (Romans 8:35) because "many live as enemies of the cross of Christ" (Philippians 3:18). Indeed, Paul tells the first believers in the Roman world a hard fact: "We must go through many hardships to enter the kingdom of God." (Acts 14:22)

This opposition continues after the age of the apostles is seen in example after example from the early church. Ignatius praised God for being counted worthy to be ripped apart by animals for the sake of Christ; Polycarp was burned for not recanting; Justin Martyr was put to death for insisting that Christians could not make sacrifices to idols. And even after Christianity became a recognized religion in the Roman Empire, Christians were often the object of criticism, persecution, defamation, and cruelty. And of course, many Christians throughout the world still experience extreme persecution and martyrdom today. In America, we may experience some degree of ridicule in various sectors, including in the workplace, schools, the political arena, and on social media. We know that behind these various forms of persecution that the Enemy works to oppose God's work; we are not unaware of his schemes (2 Corinthians 2:11).

Opposition Can Hinder Mission

It is no surprise when we look in on the story of Nehemiah that there is opposition to the mission God has given His people. The minute the people respond to Nehemiah's call to rebuild the wall, the enemies Sanballat, Tobiah, and Geshem begin their opposition. While they began with mockery, they quickly escalated their efforts, threatening harm, even leading Nehemiah to have to prepare for the possibility of military action.

Nehemiah 4 takes us into this struggle between the Jews and their enemies as Nehemiah seeks to obey the Lord in leading God's people to remove Israel's disgrace by rebuilding Jerusalem's wall. Just as Nehemiah has personal stock seeing that the mission is successful, so his enemies have personal stock in seeing that it is not. One Bible scholar explains further, "Rebuilding the walls will protect the people and create a safe place in which the law of Yahweh can be enforced, a place where justice and goodness can be upheld. This would thwart Sanballat and Tobiah because they are not interested in justice and goodness. Rather, they seek to exploit the weakness and vulnerability of the Israelites for their own profit."[7]

If Nehemiah is successful, then Israel will no longer be vulnerable to their neighbors in the same way. But as we know, when evil people sense they might lose their power, they tend to lash out in violence to scare others into submission. First with threats, then with action, this is exactly what Sanballat and Tobiah did with Nehemiah and the Jews when they found that the wall was being built and their power over the Jews was possibly coming to an end. Opposition is one of the strongest forces to potentially overthrow the mission of God's people, and the story of Nehemiah is full of such opposition (seen especially in chapters 4 and

---

7   Hamilton, Jr., *Exalting Jesus in Nehemiah*, 114.

6). Let us use the story as an opportunity to ask two important questions when it comes to external opposition: 1. In what ways do people oppose God's work? 2. How do we overcome this opposition?

Seven Ways People Oppose God's Work

1. Humiliation

Nehemiah 4:1-2, "When Sanballat heard that we were rebuilding the wall, he became angry and was greatly incensed. He ridiculed the Jews, and in the presence of his associates and the army of Samaria, he said, "What are those feeble Jews doing? Will they restore their wall? Will they offer sacrifices? Will they finish in a day? Can they bring the stones back to life from those heaps of rubble—burned as they are?"

It is not uncommon for opponents of the faith to try and humiliate or ridicule Christians for their faith. Saballat set out to ridicule the Jews, calling them "feeble" and pointing out the limited resources that they had to work with. He was seeking to remind them of their past failures, a fact evident by the fact that there were heaps of rubble from where the Babylonians had come through years ago and completely decimated the city. This is a common tactic of those who oppose the work of God's people: to deflate by drawing attention to the apparent lack of resources for the endeavor at hand and to point out past failures of which the community is ashamed. These forms of opposition are often directed against the person rather than their position in an attempt to discredit who they are. One only needs to watch the news outlets for a few minutes, especially amidst an election cycle, to see this play out today. In our context, it might look like someone trying to humiliate you because of your view of God, boldly declaring you to be dumb, unintelligent, narrowminded, and unscientific because of your views. In our time it is becoming increasingly unpopular to be a Christian with deep convictions, and so humiliation is one of the tactics we see increasingly utilized: if people are ashamed to identity with Christ and His people, they will be less able to fulfill the mission. Ultimately this is a tactic of the Enemy to discredit Christian testimony to the glory of Christ.

2. Discrimination

Nehemiah 2:10, When Sanballat the Horonite and Tobiah the Ammonite official heard about this, they were very much disturbed that someone had come to promote the welfare of the Israelites.

Discrimination is a bias against someone based on some aspect of who they are. It is often rooted in bigotry, hatred, and prejudice. We most typically think of discrimination in racial terms, but here we recognize more of a discrimination based on religious identity. These guys were disturbed simply because they were Israelites, people who worshiped the God of Israel. Sanballat was a Horonite, Tobiah was an Ammonite, Geshem was an Arab, different people groups that were neighbors of Israel and had their own set of gods that they worshipped. They represented those nations who were set in opposition to God and His purposes in the world. Why are they so disturbed by this rebuilding development? Why are they all wrapped up in what happens with this relatively small people? The reason is because they have already decided to be set against them no matter what. They lack the spiritual understanding necessary to see that the Lord Who made all the nations was doing something in and through Israel. They had already made up their minds to be against this God and His people, and there was nothing that was going to change it. Today, there is still discrimination against Christians just because they are Christians, and this has a spiritual root to it. Ask an unbeliever to describe a Christian and you will inevitably get answers such as "hypocritical," "judge," "bigots," "politically charged hate group." Some of the time these answers come from negative experiences that some people have had with professing Christians, but many times it is simply because people have decided beforehand to hate Christians and what they stand for. Discrimination is being set against what is not properly understood, and it is alive and well today as a tactic of our Enemy.

3. Demoralization

Nehemiah 4:2, "In the presence of his associates and the army of Samaria, he said, "What are those feeble Jews doing? Will they restore their wall? Will they offer sacrifices? Will they finish in a day? Can they bring the stones back to life from those heaps of rubble—burned as they are?"

Nehemiah 6:9, "They were all trying to frighten us, thinking, "Their hands will get too weak for the work, and it will not be completed."

To demoralize is to discourage, dishearten or weaken emotionally. It is not uncommon for God's people to face demoralizing attacks of those who oppose the work of God. Think about all that might have been demoralizing to Nehemiah and the Israelites in their rebuilding project: the walls had been down 140 years; the people grew weary of the task at many points and considered giving up (4:10); there was question about whether Nehemiah could really see the task to completion or if he even might have had ulterior motives; and there had to be times when the task just seemed too great. The opposition tried to play up those possibilities and discourage the people from continuing the work the Lord had called them to do. They intentionally stoke the fires of discouragement to get God's people to throw in the towel and say, "You're right: there's no way we can complete the task." Notice that demoralization often involves drawing attention to the past. For them, that meant reminders that this wall had been completely dismantled around a century and a half ago and that the place has been essentially desolate since then (remember, a defense wall was vital to a city flourishing in that time). For us, it might mean people reminding us about our past life before coming to Christ, or even things we have done since we became Christians that we are ashamed of. The past can often serve as our greatest demoralizer, for it can be so tempting to think about how horrible our past sin is and to let the voice of the enemy discourage us with that. But this is where we need to remember grace as expressed in places like Romans 8:1, "Therefore, there is now no condemnation for those who are in Christ Jesus." The battle with demoralization will be happening all the way to glory.

4. Provocation

Nehemiah 4:3, "Tobiah the Ammonite, who was at his side, said, "What they are building—even a fox climbing up on it would break down their wall of stones!"

To provoke someone is to aggravate them to anger by inciting them with hurtful claims. It is also known as "baiting" someone: trying to see if they will "bite" on a ridiculous claim and become distracted from the main thing they are trying to do. This can lead us to compromise our witness or fail to complete the work that is set before us to do. Tobiah, in Nehemiah 4:3, gives us a perfect example of provocation: he attempts to aggravate by making light of them and their effort, asserting that their work is futile, and that wall is so brittle that even a little fox clambering over it would knock it down (think about what that would mean if an enemy attacked!). This surely would have gotten Nehemiah and the people hot under the collar, and it was intended to do exactly that. Provocation often provides a test of how we will respond when someone is intentionally seeking to stir us up: are we going to let people "get our goat" or are we going to rise above their childish behavior? Instead of us stooping to their level, the New Testament calls us to shut them down with our good works. 1 Peter 2:15 says, "For it is God's will that by doing good you should silence the ignorant talk of foolish people." Romans 12:20-21 encourages us "If your enemy is hungry, feed him; if he is thirsty, give him something to drink. In doing this, you will heap burning coals on his head. Do not be overcome by evil, but overcome evil with good." This is how we *should* respond to provocation by the enemy, but doing so is easier said than done, and meanwhile provocation is one of the tools in the Enemy's tool belt to get us distracted from our mission.

5. Irritation

Nehemiah 6:2-4, "Sanballat and Geshem sent me this message: "Come, let us meet together in one of the villages on the plain of Ono." But they were scheming to harm me; so I sent messengers to them with this reply: "I am carrying on a great project and cannot go down. Why should the work stop while I leave it and go down to you?" Four times they sent me the same message, and each time I gave them the same answer."

Irritation is an attempt to distract through ongoing antagonizing. It is doing an action again and again that just rubs you raw and gets you to turn your focus away from the task at hand. Sanballat and Geshem do not actually have any business they want to do with Nehemiah (other than bringing him harm!); they request a meeting again and again to see if they can irritate Nehemiah into doing something rash, distracting him from the project of rebuilding the wall. Think about how effective this can be: if you are trying to get a task done and your children *continually* come and interrupt you and call you to help them with something, your productivity on the task at hand is going to be greatly diminished. Now, your kids do not (usually) *intend* to distract you, but in the case of these guys that is exactly their intention. Like the waves of the ocean that just continue to come in and beat your body again and again until you give up and head back to shore, so these efforts to irritate have the intention of getting Nehemiah to throw in the towel. Those who oppose God's work often won't stop until they get the result they are looking for.

6. Fabrication

Nehemiah 2:19, "But when Sanballat the Horonite, Tobiah the Ammonite official and Geshemthe Arab heard about it, they mocked and ridiculed us. "What is this you are doing?" they asked. "Are you rebelling against the king?"

Nehemiah 6:5-7, Then, the fifth time, Sanballat sent his aide to me with the same message, and in his hand was an unsealed letter in which was written: "It is reported among the nations—and Geshem says it is true—that you and the Jews are plotting to revolt, and therefore you are building the wall. Moreover, according to these reports you are about to become their king and have even appointed prophets to make this proclamation about you in Jerusalem: 'There is a king in Judah!' Now this report will get back to the king; so come, let us meet together."

Nehemiah 6:10-13, "One day I went to the house of Shemaiah son of Delaiah, the son of Mehetabel, who was shut in at his home. He said, "Let us meet in the house of God, inside the temple, and let us close the temple doors, because men are coming to kill you—by night they are coming to kill you." But I said, "Should a man like me run away? Or should someone like me go into the temple to save his life? I will not go!" I realized that God had not sent him, but that he had prophesied against me because Tobiah and Sanballat had hired him. He had been hired to intimidate me so that I would commit a sin by doing this, and then they would give me a bad name to discredit me."

Fabrication involves inventing false stories to try to cause trouble and ruin the character of their targets. We see from the very beginning of the rebuilding effort that these enemies of God's people began the work of fabrication, planting the seed that this effort is in rebellion against the king of Persia (when in fact it had the king's blessing). Once the work of rebuilding gets underway, the enemies ramp up their efforts by concocting a story that rebuilding the wall is only the first step in their rebellion against the Persians and that they intend to make Nehemiah king over Judah (which, of course, Nehemiah vehemently denies in 6:8). A third attempt at fabrication involves the invitation of Shemaiah for Nehemiah to join him in taking refuge in the temple in view of a coming attack; Nehemiah discerned that this was not only a false report (there was no pending attack) but also an attempt to discredit him before the people. Those opposed to God's work will shamelessly make up lies to forward their purpose of derailing the mission of God's people. They will tell lies about God, about us, about the world, and about the situations that we face. One very prominent example of this from early in church history is the way that Emperor Nero used Christians as a scapegoat, fabricating a story that they were the ones responsible for the great fire of 64 AD (he was the one responsible!). This unfounded accusation led to many of the Christians in Rome losing their lives in a horrific manner at the colosseum. Fabrication is dangerous because lies are easy to believe as the truth of the matter, and the result is that God's people can be detracted from the mission.

7. Intimidation

Nehemiah 4:7-9, 11-12, "When Sanballat, Tobiah, the Arabs, the Ammonites and the people of Ashdod heard that the repairs to Jerusalem's walls had gone ahead and that the gaps were being closed, they were very angry. They all plotted together to come and fight against Jerusalem and stir up trouble against it. But we prayed to our God and posted a guard day and night to meet this threat....Also our enemies said, "Before they know it or see us, we will be right there among them and will kill them and put an end to the work." Then the Jews who lived near them came and told us ten times over, "Wherever you turn, they will attack us."

Nehemiah 6:10, One day I went to the house of Shemaiah son of Delaiah, the son of Mehetabel, who was shut in at his home. He said, "Let us meet in the house of God, inside the temple, and let us close the temple doors, because men are coming to kill you—by night they are coming to kill you."

Nehemiah 6:17-19, "Also, in those days the nobles of Judah were sending many letters to Tobiah, and replies from Tobiah kept coming to them. For many in Judah were under oath to him, since he was son-in-law to Shekaniah son of Arah, and his son Jehohanan had married the daughter of Meshullam son of Berekiah. Moreover, they kept reporting to me his good deeds and then telling him what I said. And Tobiah sent letters to intimidate me."

To intimidate someone is to bully them into submission; to terrorize with threats. Nehemiah's enemies did not just conduct warfare on the psychological front; they sought to make physically intimidating remarks that would dissuade the people from continuing out of fear for their lives. We see throughout chapters 4 and 6 that because of these intimidation tactics the people must become more focused on defense, diverting some of the laborers to the role of standing guard. There were rumors and signs that the military intended to intimidate the Israelites so that they would cease the rebuilding project, fearful that continuing the labor would incur the wrath of those with power. Of course, such intimidation efforts do not have to be just physical: they can also be emotional or verbal. Some Christians throughout the world today are still intimidated physically with the threat of beatings, arrests, and even torture and death if they continue to practice their faith. In our context, the intimidation is much more likely to happen in the social arena where it is made evident that a faith perspective is not welcome and that there may be consequences (losing one's job, receiving a lower grade, not being invited to the neighborhood party) if one continues to express their Christian faith. Whatever the form of bullying, this tactic of opposition is one that God's people have faced in every age.

How Do We Overcome the Opposition?

Now that we have examined some of the opposition tactics of the Enemy, another key question emerges: how do we overcome them? If it is true that in every age there will be enemies opposed to the Gospel and seeking to disrupt the work God's people have been called to, what should we do in preparation for and response to these attacks when they come? We will look at four important principles below.

1. Know Your Enemy

Nehemiah 6:13, "He had been hired to intimidate me so that I would commit a sin by doing this, and then they would give me a bad name to discredit me."

It is important to begin by naming the work of enemies for what it is, not being naïve about the work of our enemies (and our Enemy) at work in the world. Part of what enables Nehemiah to overcome the attacks of his enemies is a discerning spirit; he is aware of what they are up to and does not fall for their attempts to veil their wicked intentions. He discerns that Sanballat, Tobiah, and Geshem seek him and God's people harm, and so he is not taken by their various efforts to distract or provoke him. He knows that Sanballat and Geshem's invitation to meet with them is a trap; he recognizes that their insistence upon a meeting is a form of distraction; he can tell that Shemaiah's invitation to hide in the temple with him is a way to discredit his reputation. How does Nehemiah know these things? Because he knows his enemies; he knows how they tick because he is a student of people and lives wisely in the world. Jesus used the image of sending his disciples out "like sheep among wolves" (Matthew 10:16). Knowing that there are wolves out there in the world seeking to do us harm sheds light on why Jesus encourages us in the same verse to "be as shrewd as snakes and as innocent as doves." Paul even says that some of these wolves are going to make it into the church, and even into leadership positions in the church. His advice in light of that: "Be on your guard!" (Acts 20:29-31). We must know that our enemies exist, and we must know their ways so that we can respond as we should. Dale Carnegie once said: "Any fool can criticize, condemn, and complain—and most fools do." If we come to know the characteristic behavior of our enemies, we will be better capable of sniffing it out and not allowing it to dissuade us from the mission at hand.

2. Keep the Faith

Nehemiah 6:15-16, "So the wall was completed on the twenty-fifth of Elul, in fifty-two days. When all our enemies heard about this, all the surrounding nations were afraid and lost their self-confidence, because they realized that this work had been done with the help of our God."

The enemy will be quite effective in preventing us from doing the work God has called us to do, if they can cause us to abandon the faith that motivates us to do that work. Essentially, our faith, our trust in God, is the center from which everything else flows, including fulfilling the mission. We can and do encounter circumstances that may *seem* to contradict that faith; when we lose someone that is very precious to us, for instance, it can *seem* that God has abandoned us or does not really love us. But we need faith as our anchor in *exactly* those moments: the moments we are under attack from an enemy. In fact, faith is choosing to live as if God's Word is true regardless of what we might want to conclude based on our circumstances, emotions, and cultural trends.

This is why Paul exhorts the church to "take up the shield of faith, with which you can extinguish all the flaming arrows of the evil one" (Ephesians 6:16). It is why the author of Hebrews encourages us to remember the "hall of faith" as a "great cloud of witnesses" so that we will be able to "throw off everything that hinders and the sin that so easily entangles.... [and] run with perseverance the race marked out for us." (Hebrews 12:1). Dorothy Bernard has said that "courage is fear that has said its prayers." Indeed, when we bring our fears about the enemy back to God in light of our faith, we see they don't have any real power over us. But if we abandon that faith, the claims and efforts of the enemy will have the power to dissuade us from the mission.

3. Focus on God

Nehemiah 4:4, "Hear us, our God, for we are despised. Turn their insults back on their own heads. Give them over as plunder in a land of captivity.

Nehemiah 4:9a, "But we prayed to our God...

Nehemiah 4:14, "After I looked things over, I stood up and said to the nobles, the officials and the rest of the people, "Don't be afraid of them. Remember the Lord, who is great and awesome..."

Nehemiah 4:20, "Wherever you hear the sound of the trumpet, join us there. Our God will fight for us!"

Nehemiah 6:9b, "But I prayed, "Now strengthen my hands"

Notice how many times Nehemiah reoriented his vision back to God, especially in prayer. He knew that for the enemy's lies not to get a foothold, he had to rehearse the promises of who God is and what He has covenanted to do for His people. It is only in light of God's infinite strength that Nehemiah doesn't have to cower at his enemy's strength; it is only in light of God's covenant promise to be with and for His people that Nehemiah can fight the lie that God has abandoned His people; it is only in light of God's grace toward sinners that Nehemiah can trust the Lord to provide deliverance even though the people are undeserving. Maintaining our focus on God, especially by hearing from Him in His Word, is central in overcoming any opposition that we face as God's people.

With our faces attentive to Him, we can ultimately never fail, even if we might falter for a moment. Thus, we take to heart Hebrews 12:2-3, which says we should fix "our eyes on Jesus, the pioneer and perfecter of faith. For the joy set before him he endured the cross, scorning its shame, and sat down at the right hand of the throne of God. Consider him who endured such opposition from sinners, so that you will not grow weary and lose heart." Indeed, when we consider that, in Jesus, God has gone before us in experiencing opposition beyond anything we will ever face, we can take great courage from His example and great encouragement from His love for us. A focus on God amidst the trials is critical!

4. Continue the Work

Nehemiah 4:9, "But we prayed to our God and posted a guard day and night to meet this threat.

Nehemiah 4:14, "After I looked things over, I stood up and said to the nobles, the officials and the rest of the people, "Don't be afraid of them. Remember the Lord, Who is great and awesome, and fight for your families, your sons and your daughters, your wives and our homes."

It might go without saying, but part of how we overcome the opposition is...we do not let the opposition stop us from our work. We keep going! This is not out of a naïve idea that it will be easy or that there will not be difficulties as we continue (that is very likely not going to be true), but that we can continue the work because it is what we know God has called us to do. Nehemiah prayed, keeping his attention focused on God; but then he got back to work, which in certain cases was posting guards in view of the threats they were receiving.

These things do not contradict each other but work in tandem with one another. Philippians 2:12-13 calls us to "continue to work out your salvation with fear and trembling" while also reminding us that "it is God who works in you to will and to act to fulfill His good purpose." God provides the power, but we still work! In fact, knowing the Lord and His power is exactly what can get us back to work, for we know we are laboring in a way that will not be in vain but will bear fruit one day. This is why Paul can say in 1 Corinthians 15:58, "Therefore, my dear brothers and sisters, stand firm. Let nothing move you. Always give yourselves fully to the work of the Lord, because you know that your labor in the Lord is not in vain." This was a good word for Nehemiah, and it is a good word for us.

5. Do not Let Your Guard Down

Nehemiah 4:16, From that day on, half of my men did the work, while the other half were equipped with spears, shields, bows and armor. The officers posted themselves behind all the people of Judah who were building the wall. Those who carried materials did their work with one hand and held a weapon in the other, and each of the builders wore his sword at his side as he worked.

At some point the work will be done. There was a day when the wall was finally complete. But for us, that work will not be done until Christ comes back. Until that moment, we will never come to a point in this life where we can say: "OK, now the attacks will stop; now the enemy is done." In fact, 1 Peter 5:9-11 promises us that our primary enemy, Satan himself, "prowls around like a roaring lion looking for someone to devour." So, continue in the effort to "Resist him, standing firm in the faith, because you know that the family of believers throughout the world is undergoing the same kind of sufferings. And the God of all grace, who called you to his eternal glory in Christ, after you have suffered a little while, will himself restore you and make you strong, firm and steadfast. To him be the power for ever and ever. Amen."

We are called to resist the devil, and yet we know that the power by which we will resist comes from God Himself. This gives us confidence to continue our efforts, not letting down our guard but rather keeping up our defensive posture so that we can continue the good work which the Lord has set before us to do. We do not let off the gas, we don't let down our guard, until glory. And then, and only then, will we enter into the rest of our Master and be able to say with Paul, "I have fought the good fight, I have finished the race, I have kept the faith. Now there is in store for me the crown of righteousness, which the Lord, the righteous Judge, will award to me on that day—and not only to me, but also to all who have longed for his appearing." (2 Timothy 4:7-8)

Next Steps

Where do we go from here? Part of what this chapter should do is make us more aware of the fact that there are enemies out there, looking to detract us from the mission, led by the Enemy who is looking to "steal, kill and destroy" (John 10:10). We do not need to fear these enemies; we know their power has *nothing* on the power of our God! But we do want to be aware of their schemes; we want to be wise and shrewd as serpents as we make our way through this world that is set against God and His purposes.

Spend some time reflecting on where you think the Enemy might be at work through opposition that you face in your life. Maybe it is the temptation to stop connecting with believers amidst the global pandemic; maybe it is reticence to be generous because you are afraid you will not have enough money for retirement; maybe it is a concern to share the faith with your neighbors because of the potential social cost. Whatever opposition that you face to aligning with the mission which God has given the church, bring that opposition before God's throne in prayer and recognize that He will provide you everything you need to overcome that opposition.

He provided it to Nehemiah and the Israelites so many years before. Nehemiah and the Jewish people completed the wall in just over fifty days' time, working day and night to complete their mission and the will of God. All odds were against them, yet they succeeded because of God's grace and faithfulness. Christians have access to the same powerful, gracious, and faithful God. The God of the Old Testament is the same God Who has revealed Himself in Christ and in the New Testament. He promises to do the same thing for His people today.

When believers faithfully obey God, He provides for them the strength and perseverance to succeed in otherwise impossible circumstances. We do not need to fear opposition of any sort. All the intimidations and manipulations of the world are mere droplets in the infinite ocean of God's faithfulness and might. Therefore, we must remain courageous and resolved in our faithfulness to God and His Word. Only then can Christians endure opposition and claim the victory in our mission to glorify God and share the true Gospel with the lost.

Prayer: God of all power and might, I praise You that no opposition against Your people could ever stand, because You have told us that even the gates of Hell will never prevail against Your Church. I pray for greater faith to rebuke the enemies of my life with the truth of Your Word. I pray for courage to face any opposition out of the power that the Holy Spirit provides to me. And I pray that You would keep me attentive to the mission You have given me, that it might be accomplished for Your glory. In Jesus' name I pray...Amen.

Chapter 5: Maintain Your Focus

Read Nehemiah 9:1-36

Big Picture

How do we rebuild a life that matters? By maintaining our focus on who God wants us to be as we rebuild. We must grow in being honest with ourselves, with others, and with God, continually confessing our sin, repenting of ways that we have fallen short, and offering up all our lives in worship as we carry out the mission.

A Need to Focus

Maintaining your focus in life is especially important to becoming who God wants you to be. We can get off to a great start in the project of rebuilding our lives, and yet losing our focus somewhere along the line prevents that work from coming to its intended completion. In other words, we cannot just start well in the work of being renewed for the mission God has for us; we also must continue well by remaining focused on what the Lord desires us to do and who He desires us to be. If our focus is in the right place, a lot of other things will work out just fine. But if we lose our focus on the first things, our whole life can quickly fall apart.

I have seen this illustrated from an experience in my own family. Several years ago, my oldest son Jace was sitting at the Thanksgiving table and one of his eyes turned in. As new parents, my wife and I were extremely concerned. We called our doctor and he arranged for us to meet with a specialist immediately. Those were nerve racking days.

The diagnosis turned out to be simple—he had extremely poor vision, and his eyes were unable to properly focus. He was prescribed glasses and I remember thinking to myself, "This rough and tumble boy is never going to wear glasses." However, to my surprise, he embraced them immediately. Why? Because for the first time in his life he was able to focus, and everything else came into place after that. The first morning after he received his glasses he walked into our bedroom and he already had his glasses on! It shocked us. He was finally able to focus, and this enabled him to live the kind of life he was designed to live. We also have a need to focus, not just visually, but spiritually. We need to keep our focus on God and His intentions for us to live the kind of life that He desires all the way to glory.

Why We Do Not Focus

Of course, staying focused is easy to say, but hard to do. Why is that? Because there are so many things out there that are competing for our attention, and are attempting to take our attention off Christ. The truth is, we are far too easily distracted by "something shiny" that makes us take our focus off God and on to other things that will not be good for us to base our lives on. In the Christian life we need to learn how to say "no" to these distractions, and to even starve these distractions so we can properly maintain our focus on God.

This is a discipline, something that we learn how to do through practice over a long period of time. Our fallen default mode is to jump from one thing to the next (as our behavior surfing the web makes evident!). It has been said that the successful person is the average person with laser-like focus. Winston Churchill once said that "You will never reach your destination if you stop and throw stones at every dog that barks." He is saying that we will never get where we are trying to go if we do not stay focused. In fact, I like the acronym FOCUS: Follow One Course Until Successful. That one course, for the believer, is being made more and more into Christ's image and be found fully mature in Him (Colossians 1:28) so we can complete the mission He has given the church.

In Nehemiah 9, after the work of rebuilding the wall is complete, you might think the Israelites would be taking a victory lap, celebrating their accomplishment and the way they overcame the opposition (hooray!). Instead, we essentially find Israel's leaders imploring the children of God to stay focused. In the preceding chapters, we learned that Nehemiah had joined up with Ezra to help the people be attentive to God and what God had said in His Word. In chapter 9, we watch as the history of God's people is recounted as a reminder: stay focused on who you really are and what work you are continually called to (now that the wall rebuilding is done). In many ways, the leaders insist, the real work was just starting: the work not of rebuilding a wall, but the work of rebuilding their lives and their community as dedicated solely to God.

One Bible scholar lays out seven distinct sections in this prayer that we are going to be looking at:

1. Praise to God as Creator (Nehemiah 9:6), perhaps reflecting the fact that in recent weeks the people have been listening to the reading of the first five books of the Old Testament, beginning with the story of creation in Genesis 1.

2. A record of God's power and grace right up to that day (the twenty-fourth day of the month of Tishri, 444 B.C.) against a backdrop of the Israelites' repeated failure during their forty-year period of wandering in the wilderness (Nehemiah 9:7–15). They recall especially that, despite the provision of food and water and protection, they refused to listen to God and tried to return to Egypt (v. 16).

3. A testimony to God's forgiveness, graciousness, and compassion in memorable words: "You are a God ready to forgive, gracious and merciful, slow to anger and abounding in steadfast love, and did not forsake them" (Nehemiah 9:17). Throughout this period, they "lacked nothing" (v. 21); God met their every need.

4. An open confession of sin (Nehemiah 9:26–31). The prayer records the period of the judges and the monarchy with characteristic summaries of sin on their part and grace on God's part: "They were disobedient.... You are a gracious and merciful God" (vv. 26, 31).

5. A resting in God's covenant faithfulness: "the great, the mighty, and the awesome God, who keeps covenant and steadfast love" (Nehemiah 9:32).

6. A complaint that the people are in distress; they are "slaves" or "servants" (Nehemiah 9:36; both translations are possible) under Persian rule—and if the former, a

daring acknowledgment given that Ezra and Nehemiah were both civil servants of this regime.

7. A solemn, climactic oath and recommitment by way of covenant reaffirmation: "Because of all this we make a firm covenant in writing; on the sealed document are the names of our princes, our Levites, and our priests" (Nehemiah 9:38).[8] Let's now look at some specifics of this passage and how they set forth six ways to maintain spiritual focus.

Six Ways to Maintain Spiritual Focus

1. Confess Your Sins Regularly

Nehemiah 9:1-2, "On the twenty-fourth day of the same month, the Israelites gathered together, fasting and wearing sackcloth and putting dust on their heads. Those of Israelite descent had separated themselves from all foreigners. They stood in their places and confessed their sins and the sins of their ancestors."

There is an adage in business about "keeping short accounts." The idea of keeping short accounts means that you should pay your debts and receive payoffs quickly. Well, it turns out we can say the same about our sin. We should confess our sins consistently and regularly—in other words, keeping short accounts with God. This is what we see in Nehemiah chapter 9. The Israelites gather for the purpose of confessing their sin, which means that they are in the habit of doing so to some extent. The Israelites and

---

8   Derek Thomas, *Ezra & Nehemiah* ed. R. D. Phillips, P. G. Ryken, & I. M. Duguid, REC (Phillipsburg, NJ: P&R Publishing, 2016), 355-356.

their leaders realized that sin was both a past and present problem. Their ancestors had brought trouble on themselves because of sin. They also realized that they were not free from the clutches of sin, even if they were able to experience the victory of a rebuilt wall.

Confessing our sins is not just something we do when we become Christians; it is something we do throughout the Christian life. When it comes to repentance, there is no hiding and no strategy for sin management: God already knows *all* of what you thought, said, and did. He knows you and your heart (way!) better than you do. So, the best course of action is to come clean with Him immediately and as often as we need to. We know that when we come before God with a contrite and repentant heart, He holds no forgiveness back because of Jesus' work on our behalf. That is how gracious God is, and that is our great hope when we confess to Him.

Confession may seem like a frightening task, but when we remember that we are simply confessing to our Heavenly Father Who loves us in Christ, we can call out to Him without fear. In fact, it has been observed that this is the main difference between religion and Christianity. When we sin, religion says: "I hope my Father doesn't find out; He'll be so upset" while the Gospel says, "I need to call my Father; I know He'll forgive me." This is based on the promise of 1 John 1:9 "If we confess our sins, he is faithful and just and will forgive us our sins and purify us from all unrighteousness." We know He will forgive our sins that we confess because He has already demonstrated His love for us while we were still sinners, sending His Son to take our place on the cross. This is a truth worth singing, as we do in the great hymn of the faith: "Grace Greater than All Our Sin." In it we sing: "Grace, Grace, God's Grace, Grace that will pardon and cleanse within; Grace, Grace, God's Grace, Grace that is greater than all our sin." Amen!

But even though we know this to be the case, it can still be hard to confess our sins. Very hard! There is, after all, perhaps nothing more painful than admitting that you have done something wrong, that you are the one who messed up (bigtime!). I mean, having to approach someone (like my wife!) whom I have wronged and say, "I'm sorry" is probably one of the hardest things for me to do. Two words: "I'm" "Sorry."

These words should roll off the tongue so easily, but they so often do not because the truth is that saying these words involves a cost. When you utter an apology, when you confess, you give part of yourself away, the part that was holding onto your justification for the wrongdoing, the part that was trying to hide the wrongdoing, the part that was trying to maybe flip the wrongdoing onto someone else. But our God, Who is (amazingly given how much we sin!) slow to anger and abounding in love, has given us reason to say those words to Him. He is gracious, merciful, patient with us. This is our God, and this is the God to Whom the Israelites confess in Nehemiah 9. Let us press into the habit, the discipline, of confessing our sins regularly, for as St. Augustine has said, we know "God gives [forgiveness] where He finds empty hands.

2. Read God's Word Daily

Nehemiah 9:3, "They stood where they were and read from the Book of the Law of the LORD their God for a quarter of the day."

Israel's leaders, including Nehemiah, understood that the best way for the children of Israel not to repeat the mistakes of their ancestors was to read God's Word to the people and to help them understand what it meant and what it looked like to live in light of it. They understood that even after such an incredible experience as rebuilding a wall in 52 days, they were still prone to repeat the error of the forbears. In fact, isn't it true that after the greatest "spiritual highs" of our lives (maybe attending an exhilarating camp, going on an international mission trip, or seeing a close friend or family member come to Christ) we are most in danger of experiencing the "spiritual letdown" when we get back to our normal life? The best way to fight against that slump and to keep our focus is to get into a pattern of daily Bible reading.

But we can say more. Notice in this passage, that as Israel's leaders are imploring the children of Israel to stay focused on God, they recount the history of what God has done (recorded in the Bible!) for His people despite their sin and rebellion. For instance, look at Nehemiah 9:9-15 and notice how many verbs shows us God's focus on and care for Israel even though they were often hard-hearted and far from the Lord: God saw, heard, sent, divided, led, came down, delivered, made known, fed, brought, and gave, all to care for Israel.

The Word reveals that He acted graciously on their behalf, and that is a great summary of the whole Bible: God acting graciously on behalf of a people who do not deserve it. When we read the Bible daily, we are not just reading to learn *information*; we are reading to be *reminded* of who we are, who God is, and what God has done for His people though there is nothing we have done to deserve it. In short, even when we are reading the Bible, our focus should continually be upon God and what we learn about Him from the Scriptures.

Reading God's Word regularly reminds us of past victories and failures while also shedding light on our future. In Romans 15:4 Paul tells us what the purpose of Scripture is. He says, "For everything that was written in the past was written to teach us, so that through the endurance taught in the Scriptures and the encouragement they provide we might have hope." In fact, in 1 Corinthians 10:11 Paul says that the things which occurred to

God's people in the past are examples for us "written down as warnings for us..."

We see that Paul believes Scripture is a great teacher, a living and active Word rather than a dead letter. It teaches us that God was active not only in the glorious events of Israel's history, like the Exodus, but also in the lives of individuals, like Nehemiah. Scripture teaches us that God uses individuals like him, who are both flawed and favored. In fact, the spiritual giants of Scripture clearly have their warts; think about the way Abraham feared those in power, or the rashness exhibited by Moses, or the adultery and murder (!) committed by David.

Paul says these things were written for us, to help us understand that when we fail (and we will fail), God is compassionate when we turn back to Him and ask for forgiveness. Scripture provides us the means we need to endure in the faith. After all, life is not easy. Trials and difficulties do come, but if we are drinking regularly from Scripture we will be thoroughly equipped to press on and trust God, not letting the distractions take our eye off the prize.

In short, reading God's Word keeps us focused. It helps us avoid the distractions in our daily lives by focusing us again and again on the things that really matter: God and what God has done in Christ by the Spirit to redeem a fallen creation, including each of us. Reading God's Word gives us hope for the future in a largely hopeless world.

As the Psalmist said in Psalm 119:105, "Your word is a lamp for my feet, a light on my path." The imagery could not be clearer: too often we walk in darkness and doubt. We do not know what to do today, much less in our future. But God's Word provides the lamp that we need, giving us the ability to focus on Him and the hope that He provides us in this life and the next. The light reminds us that God has a wonderful plan for our future (Jeremiah 29:11).

3. Worship God Only

Nehemiah 9:3, "They...spent another quarter...in worshipping the Lord their God."

When we read the Word, not only will we be promoted to confess our sin (back to #1 above), but we will also be drawn into a deeper worship of God and of Him alone. Derek Thomas writes, "He is "the Lord their God" (Nehemiah 9:3–4), Who revealed Himself to them in covenant (v. 32). In an age when, as David Wells puts it, we seem to be persuaded of the "weightlessness of God," Ezra and his companions are overwhelmed by God's greatness. This is precisely what Jesus exemplifies in His response to the disciples' request for help in prayer. He gives them the model of the Lord's Prayer, in which the first half extols the Father's glory and greatness. He was urging them to focus on God."[9]

Israel's leaders understood that worship of God alone was another key to keeping focused. Worship is adoration of another (reserved for God alone) and is often characterized by quietness, humility, bowing and kneeling before God. We will look at praise below, which is slightly different in that praise is something we can give to lots of things (like our spouse, our coworkers, etc.), but worship is something we give only to God.

Praise can be a part of worship, but worship goes beyond praise. Worship gets to the heart of who we are. True worship keeps us from worshipping idols, things we look to as substitutes for God that we believe will provide ultimate satisfaction and purpose. Idols are not just wooden statues; they can be powerful

---

9   Thomas, 357.

things like money, comfort, sexual satisfaction, or prestige. Scripture is full of exhortations to worship God and God alone, such as Jesus' rebuke of Satan in Luke 4:8 when He said, "It is written: 'Worship the Lord your God and serve him only.'" Psalm 95:6 invites us to "Come, let us bow down in worship, let us kneel before the LORD our Maker." And Exodus 20:3 makes it clear that proper worship is exclusive: "You shall have no other gods before me."

This passage reminds us that the God we worship is the God Who is powerful enough to create everything that is but also gracious enough to make a covenant with an undeserving people. God is the One Who created the heavens and the earth, the One Who ordained the seasons (Genesis 1:14-19). He is almighty and powerful. Yet, this same God can be called upon here as "our God." The almighty Creator of all is also the Israelites' God. They can claim Him as their own. And of course, because of Christ, we can too.

Paul claims that the mystery has been revealed that "through the gospel the Gentiles are heirs together with Israel, members together of one body, and sharers together in the promise in Christ Jesus" (Ephesians 3:6). We, too, can claim the God of all creation as "our God." When we pray the Lord's prayer, we can say, "*Our Father*, Who art in Heaven, hallowed by Thy name."

Worship properly mixes awe at who God is with awe at what God has mercifully done for us. It is what helps us maintain a Godward focus that can illuminate every single day of our lives. Let us resolve to take a few moments every day, from this day onward, to meditate on how great God is and how loving and kind He is to us. When we are tempted to find worldly solutions for our discomfort and suffering, God calls us to press deeper into Him so we can experience His grace more fully. He calls us to worship.

4. Praise God and Others Consistently

Nehemiah 9:5, "And the Levites...said: "Stand up and praise the Lord your God, who is from everlasting to everlasting."

A key distinction between worship and praise in Scripture is seen through the Bible. Whereas worship is often accompanied by a quietness before God, praise is anything but quiet. The number of times God's people are exhorted to praise the Lord in the Bible are too numerous to count. Psalm 150:1-6 is illustrative in its exhortation again and again: praise! It says "Praise the LORD. Praise God in His sanctuary; praise Him in His mighty heavens. Praise Him for His acts of power; praise Him for His surpassing greatness. Praise Him with the sounding of the trumpet, praise Him with the harp and lyre, praise Him with timbrel and dancing, praise Him with the strings and pipe, praise Him with the clash of cymbals, praise Him with resounding cymbals. Let everything that has breath praise the LORD. Praise the LORD." Here in our passage, the Levites are calling the Israelites to praise God for who He is and particularly for what He has done in enabling the wall to be successfully rebuilt.

Of course, others may be praised as well for the way they have acted in accordance with God's standards. We are encouraged in Scripture to praise others often. If you are married, you want to praise your spouse for the good things they have done and achieved. As parents, we should praise our children often. As employers or employees, we want to praise those in our places of work for the good things they have done. Praise of both God and others is biblical and an important part of our lives.

Praise is inherently joyful and loud, and so we are called to join the chorus of God's people through the ages to give praise (often with musical accompaniment) to God for who He is and what He has done. Look at how Psalm 145:4-10 makes it clear that this act of praise is intergenerational. It says "One generation commends Your works to another; they tell of Your mighty acts. They speak of the glorious splendor of Your majesty—and I will meditate on Your wonderful works. They tell of the power of Your awesome works— and I will proclaim Your great deeds. They celebrate Your abundant goodness and joyfully sing of Your righteousness. The LORD is gracious and compassionate, slow to anger and rich in love. The LORD is good to all; He has compassion on all He has made. All Your works praise You, LORD; Your faithful people extol You." Notice the important back and forth here: as the current generation hears the praises of the previous generation, it sparks the current generation to participate even more, recognizing in a deeper way that all of God's faithful people extol Him and spur one another on to extol Him more!

Also, did you see in Psalm 150 above that it is loud both in vocalization and instrumentation? Giving praise is not something we should sleep through! It is something we should actively engage in with a spiritual fever accompanied by both volume and veracity. Praise is the *joyful* recounting of all God has done for us. It is closely intertwined with thanksgiving as we offer back to God appreciation for His mighty works on our behalf. Since God has done many wonderful deeds, He is *worthy* of praise (Psalm 18:3). Praise is not just for Sunday worship. True praise is an everyday experience because praise is simply recognizing that reality that everywhere we turn we encounter the amazing works of our God.

Here we might ask one more question. What about the times when it is *hard* to praise due to the circumstances of our lives? The person who has lost their spouse or gone months and months without finding a job may find that praise is happening a lot less spontaneously. Is all hope lost? No. Even in this passage, we see that praise is happening amidst difficulty and lament. Despite the exciting development of the rebuilt wall, the people recognize in Nehemiah 9:26-37 that "we are slaves today, slaves in the land you gave our ancestors....Because of our sins, its abundant harvest goes to the kings you have placed over us. They rule over our bodies and our cattle as they please. We are in great distress." The Jews still lived under the auspices of the Persian king, but their desire was to live only under the God of their ancestors. They lamented that in many ways they were under the power of a foreign ruler. But part of what this lament does is lead them to long for the day when they will praise God for His *future* deliverance, the day when their "great distress" is over. When you walk through the "great distresses" of your life, remember that God's character and covenant promises remain the same. He is worthy of praise now, and one day, when the cloud lifts for you (and it will again one day), you will see that clearly once again, and it will lead you into a deeper praise of God than you would have experienced without your time of trial.

5. Obey God Purposefully

Nehemiah 9:16, "But they, our ancestors, became arrogant and stiff-necked, and they did not obey your commands. They refused to listen and failed to remember the miracles you performed among them..."

This passage points out again and again that all the troubles that came upon the children of Israel were because they lost focus on God and started focusing on themselves. We see the Israelites described here as arrogant, stiff-necked, disobedient, and rebellious, and we see that the calamities which befell them in their history can be traced back to the fact that they did not obey what the Lord had commanded them. Even after God came and showed

His grace and compassion, the children of Israel would forget and lose their focus on God all over again. And once we lose our focus on God, the ability to obey Him falls quickly to the wayside.

Perhaps this same experience has happened to you. You know there are days way back there in your life where you know God showed up in a big way and brought abundant blessing and favor. But it is so easy for those days to feel so far in the rearview mirror that you have essentially forgotten them and thus are struggling to obey God because of a lack of focus on Him.

What now? First, remember what the Israelites were told here: "But you are a forgiving God, gracious and compassionate, slow to anger and abounding in love. Therefore, you did not desert them" (Nehemiah 9:17). What an encouragement that is—regardless of how far we have drifted from God and how much we have turned away from Him and towards our own selfish behavior—God is still gracious. Not only is God gracious, but He is also faithful where we are faithless (Nehemiah 9:33). This is what kicks us in gear for obedience because true obedience only flows out of thanksgiving for what has been done. In the Gospel, we obey because we are already accepted, not in order to be accepted.

If we are honest, the word "obey" has a bad rap today. In our country, we tend to emphasize that we are the "land of the free," and thus we can live any way we want, move anywhere we want, and say whatever we want. This does not leave a lot of room for talk about "obedience," or any other restriction of our behavior from someone in authority. Therefore, it is so tough for parents to ask their kids to obey, for teachers to make their students obey, for police officers to exercise authority over criminals, and so on.

Today, obedience is out, and freedom is in. However, Nehemiah understood very clearly that for the children of Israel, obedience to God was true freedom, because it was the key to not repeating the failures of the past and living in the way that God has created us to live. Nehemiah understood, as we should, that obedience to God is the way to true freedom, and that obeying God is another way that we continually stay focused on what He wants us to do.

Deep down we know that obeying God means following commands which are always for my own good. We know this because we have laws in our own land that govern our actions and behavior, that restrict what we can do, that take away our freedom, and we see this as a good thing. We are not free to steal cars or evade taxes or slug somebody we do not like, and we all think we are a better place because we have laws against these things.

We understand that the more we follow these laws, the more peaceful and prosperous our society will be. When people break these laws, problems inevitably follow. This is a picture of how it is in God's world in general: the more we obey His commands, the more our families, neighborhoods, and personal lives will succeed. The more we obey God's laws the more we will find fulfillment and joy in our lives.

Now, this does not mean that you must track down all the laws of God in Scripture and then try to follow them judiciously one by one...it has already been tried, and it did not go so well. Instead, we can rejoice that Jesus simplified God's law for us in Matthew 22:37-40. To the question of the greatest command "Jesus replied: "'Love the Lord your God with all your heart and with all your soul and with all your mind.' This is the first and greatest commandment. And the second is like it: 'Love your neighbor as yourself.' All the Law and the Prophets hang on these two commandments." In these two laws, you have all the others.

Beautiful, isn't it? Instead of being overwhelmed with a list of rules, we are freed up to obey God by asking whether anything that we are doing is done out of love for God and for others. So, in seeking to keep our focus on God, you can ask yourself two very simple questions daily: 1) Am I demonstrating a love for God in my actions, and 2) am I showing love for others in my words and deeds? If the answer to those question is yes, you can be assured you are walking in obedience. If the answer is no, then confess your sins and ask for help in walking in a manner that is in keeping with these two great commands.

6. Repeat This Process Constantly

Nehemiah 9:38, "In view of all this, we are making a binding agreement, putting it in writing, and our leaders, our Levites and our priests are affixing their seals to it."

The march to spiritual maturity and faithfulness is more than a one-time event. We never arrive in the work of becoming more like Christ. Rather, we must continue in the habits of godliness again and again and again. Confession, reading God's Word, worship, praise, and obedience are not one-time activities; they are lifetime activities. They should become part of our daily life so that each day we wake up and do them again as if they are second nature.

The Israelites realized that they needed something to help them remember to walk through this same cycle again and again. So, they made a covenant, a binding agreement, as a way of reminding themselves of their daily commitment to stay focused on God. They "made *a solemn promise to live wholeheartedly for God whatever the cost.* It is an act of collective consecration. This is a spirit that we should all long for. Do you not long for such a spirit as this? Are you not tired of living with one foot in the world and one foot in the kingdom of God? Does your heart not long to break free from unproductive days of spiritual lethargy to experience a time of nearness to God? And do you not long for this not only for yourself, but also for the entire church? Oh, that God's Spirit would come down and take hold of us in similar fashion!"[10] This commitment was made for their spiritual revival, and would a similar commitment do the same for us!

The book of Nehemiah reminds us that the process matters. The act of making a binding agreement and putting it in writing makes it easy to follow and repeat consistently. Sometimes we are suspicious of formal commitments and systematic processes, afraid that they will take the spirit out and make everything rote observation. But in fact, formal commitments help us to be more likely to succeed. Processes, systematic series of actions that are directed to some purposeful end, help us to stay focused in God by repeating things again and again and again. It is why a Bible reading plan can often be such a help; if I have a plan already in place for what part of the Bible, I am going to read every day, I am more likely to read the Bible any particular day. As Christ-followers, we need a laser-like focus that comes from constantly repeating the process of confession, Word, worship, praise, and obedience. This process helps takes things from a one-time desire that quickly fades to a deep-seated discipline that is with us our whole life.

Next Steps

What we are saying is that the practices of the Christian life are a lot like taking a shower: doing it just once is not going to cut it! We need to "wash, rinse, repeat" throughout our lives, rather than just when we feel like it (let us especially remind our middle school boys of this one!). And we also have a formula for the focused Christian life, something like "Confess, Read, Worship, Praise, Obey, Repeat." Once we have embedded this process in our daily routines, we will have so many things working for us that

---

10   Thomas, 359.

help us to remain focused on the Lord. Our lives will be marked by disciplines we can't help but do: kneel and confess, sit and read, bow and worship, stand and praise, walk in obedience, and do it all over again the next day

The picture which emerges from our passage is of the bride of Christ pleading: "I want this marriage to work, and the fault has been all mine! Please forgive me! You have every right to throw me out and have nothing to do with me ever again, but I want us to start anew. Whatever I have done, I *do* love you." [11] Such pleas show that the bride recognizes the grace that has been extended by the husband. But the plea of true love only becomes believable if there are corresponding actions. It is these actions that we are seeking to cultivate in our lives so that we can remain focused on God and the mission which He has for us. What do you need to do, what patterns and habits do you need to commit to, to grow in that focus on Christ?

Prayer: Lord, will You show me where I need to continue to cultivate a focus on You? I need You to come and cultivate in me a desire to confess my sins, to read Your Word, to worship You alone, to praise You as you deserve, and to obey what You have commanded. Like the ancient Israelites, apart from You I can do nothing. Apart from Your grace, all of these are mere human acts that have no lasting power. But with You, these things can become part of my daily life. May it be so more and more to Your glory. In Jesus' name I pray...Amen.

---

11   Thomas, 357.

Chapter 6: Stay Committed

Read Nehemiah 10:28-39, 13:1-31

Big Picture

How do we rebuild a life that matters? By staying committed to the Lord and to the mission all the way to the end, even amidst setbacks. In order to have a life truly rebuilt by God, we need to be committed to His rebuilding project all the way to glory. In order to do that, we need to identify clear pathways to stay committed.

The Need to Staying Committed

As we close the book of Nehemiah, we see glimpses of hope and glimpses of despair. We see a reaffirmation of commitment to God in chapter 10. Hopes are high that this time Israel is going to get it right; this time the commitment is going to stick. One can imagine something like the lyrics from the hymn "Who Is On the Lord's Side?" being sung that day with confidence: "Who is on the Lord's side? Who will serve the King? Who will be His helpers, other lives to bring? Who will leave the world's side? Who will face the foe? Who is on the Lord's side? Who for Him will go? By thy call of mercy, by thy grace divine, we are on the Lord's side—Savior, we are thine!" They were riding high off the victory of the rebuilt wall and the corporate gatherings of celebration, repentance, and the hearing of God's Word. There was electricity in the air.

Until there wasn't. After chapters 11 and 12 provide us more technical information about the families who resided in Jerusalem and those who served as priests and Levities, we see in chapter 13 that the commitment had slipped away almost as soon as their leaders left. The last chapter of the book feels anticlimactic: after all of the struggle and the victory and the movements of God and the grand promises of the people, we find Nehemiah back in Jerusalem cleaning up several messes which indicate the people had not kept their promises: the Sabbath was desecrated, the temple grounds and equipment was mismanaged, and there was intermarriage with the surrounding nations, among other problems.

It looks as if the reforms of the last few chapters are an abject failure. It might be easy at this point for us to chime in and say "Wow, I can't believe those Israelites did it again! How could they have been so faithless?" But the reality is that the situation at the end of Nehemiah 13 is closer to our situation than we might want to think. The people of Nehemiah's day are more similar to us than we might want to admit.

We all struggle with commitment, with seeing things through to the very end. Yet, commitment is vital: from marriage to the work world, commitment is rightly held at a premium. How much more so when we talk about commitment to the God Who has redeemed us. So, the critical question is, how do we keep our commitments when we make them? How do we stay the course of rebuilding our lives all the way to the end?

The Road to Staying Committed

One of the things we recognize in answering this question is that it is not enough to just have *individual* practices which keep us focused on God (which we examined in the last chapter). It is just as important to have *corporate* practices which help us to stay the course. Notice that in Nehemiah 10:28-29 the picture is that everyone is involved in making this covenantal commitment: "The rest of the people—priests, Levites, gatekeepers, musicians, temple servants... together with their wives and all their sons and daughters who are able to understand—all these now join their fellow Israelites the nobles, and bind themselves with a curse and an oath." They were all in this together, and the same is true for us. The church, the community of God's people today, is in this together, called to help each other stay the course.

It is also worth noting that their covenant renewal was *specific*. It did not just offer a broad statement of intent; it also got down to brass tacks, offering a series of very detailed stipulations for what it would look like to keep this commitment before the Lord (and which Nehemiah can point to in chapter 13 to show exactly where they had fallen short). Specificity is important when making promises.

Think about marriage vows; while it may sound fine at first for them to simply express a vague notion of love, it is actually much better to have the specific situations of commitment in view: "for richer, for poorer, in sickness and in health, so long as we both shall live." The same is true here: specific covenant obligations provide important guardrails that keep God's people on the straight and narrow. Indeed, one Bible scholar notes that there are five specific areas of obedience which are clearly laid out: marriage (Nehemiah 10:30), the Sabbath (v. 31), a temple tax for maintaining worship (v. 32), a curious statement about firewood for the "wood offering" (v. 34), and offerings of various kinds (vv. 35–39).[12] While the specific areas of obligation have changed in the New Covenant, the reality that we do better with more specific guardrails has not.

Commitment is hard. We are prone to experiencing short bursts of dedication to God, but committing to something long-term, having long-term faith and zealousness, is problematic for many of us. One could say we have "commitment issues." If we are going to rebuild our lives in a way that really brings about lasting change, we have to take these head on so that we don't find ourselves in a Nehemiah 13 scenario: a lot of talk, but not much to show for it. Let's look at the five commitments that they made and discuss how these can help us envision what staying committed to the Lord would look like.

Five Commitments They Made:

1. To Live According to God's Word

Nehemiah 10:29, "…to follow the Law of God given through Moses the servant of God and to obey carefully all the commands, regulations and decrees of the LORD our Lord."

This is the foundational commitment: to let the Word of God be what sets the vision for all of life, out of the conviction that these are God's words and God knows what is best. The commitment to live according to God's Word involved specifically here a commitment to obedience. Nehemiah specifically records the Jews' intention to "enter into a curse and an oath to walk in God's Law that was given by Moses the servant of God, and to observe

---

12   Thomas, 366.

and do all the commandments of the Lord our Lord and his rules and his statutes" (Nehemiah 10:29). Their promise is with respect to *God's* law, not *man's* law....The desire of a believer to render obedience to the Ten Commandments out of gratitude for grace received is what God expects and what Spirit-filled believers wholeheartedly desire."[13] This is the proper path for the Christian today: desiring to carefully obey the commands of God because of what God has graciously done for us in Christ. It is not obeying commands to be saved; it is obey commands because one is saved.

2. To Walk In Purity

Nehemiah 10:30, "We promise not to give our daughters in marriage to the peoples around us or take their daughters for our sons.

Here we need to recognize that in the Old Covenant, God had set Israel apart from the nations around it in order that they could live distinctive lives that would testify to the watching world what it looked like for a people to live according to God's way. In order for their life together to be distinctive, they couldn't have any outside influence, because that influence would inevitably lead to compromise in terms of what the Lord required from His people in their proper worship of Him.

Other nations had other gods, and other ways they thought God was supposed to be worshipped (even through atrocities like child sacrifice or temple prostitution). So, here it must be understood that the ban on marrying foreigners was for religious protection and not out of an ethnic elitism. There are no grounds for promoting one people group as being any better or worse than any other; all stand in equal need of Christ's work and all are able to be incorporated into the multinational Body of Christ, the Church.

---

13   Thomas, 365-366.

The commitment here was to walk in purity as the Lord had commanded them to by not intermarrying with the nations that could compromise their true worship of God as He had instructed.

Of course, even though we no longer have any restrictions on who we can marry (other than that they should be another believer, 2 Corinthians 6:14-18), the common bond is that Christian marriages are supposed to be different, set apart, holy unto God. We too are called to walk in purity, in our marriage relationship and in preparation for our marriage relationship should the Lord call us to that. All of God's people, single and married, husbands and wives, are to live lives of purity as He has directed us in His Word.

3. To Remember the Sabbath

Nehemiah 10:31, "When the neighboring peoples bring merchandise or grain to sell on the Sabbath, we will not buy from them on the Sabbath or on any holy day.

God had given the Jewish people very specific instructions about how they were to worship Him, and one part of that which was very significant was observing Sabbath rest and keeping the Sabbath day holy. The Sabbath was central as one of the key ways that God's people were set apart from the nations, with the Sabbath being the primary sign and seal of the Mosaic covenant. It was so central it was the fourth of the Ten Commandments, and it was grounded in the fact that God Himself rested on the seventh day of Creation. To keep the Sabbath was to follow God's very specific instructions about how He was to be worshipped and to imitate God in what He modeled in creating the world. It was a way for Israel to have a day set aside to worship the Lord, one where work or the daily burdens would not harass.

Now, we don't keep Sabbath in the same way as the Jewish people, if only because we actually gather on Sundays as the Lord's Day, the day Jesus rose from the grave. But one Bible scholar helps us by encouraging us to see at least one point of contacts: "At the very least, we should attempt to keep [a day] holy—*different* from the rest of the week—by refraining from unnecessary labor and commerce and maintaining a weekly attendance at church along with our brothers and sisters. It remains a witness in a godless society that the lights are on and the parking lot is full at the local church on Sunday morning and evening!"[14] Having a day marked out for rest and worship, to be able to put away the work that drives us the other six days of the week, is a real blessing if we can embrace it as such.

4. To Serve Alongside God's People

Nehemiah 10:34, "We—the priests, the Levites and the people— have cast lots to determine when each of our families is to bring to the house of our God at set times each year a contribution of wood to burn on the altar of the LORD our God, as it is written in the Law.

We see a strong commitment to serving with the whole community and not as lone rangers. In fact, this passage paints a beautiful picture of community and how everyone is really connected in worshipping God together. What God has said in His Word has implications for how families function; it has implications for how the generations contribute; it has implications for different roles that different parts of Israel (such as Levites) were to play in relationship to each other. God cares not just about how individuals live, but how communities function, and whether they function together, in harmony. God uses various vocations, such

---

14   Thomas, 369.

as artistry and musical giftings, to make distinctive contributions to the worship efforts of the people. The picture is that everyone has something to contribute, and everyone needs everyone else to contribute.

Of course, this is all the more true today. Paul paints the image of the church as body with many parts, each of which is distinct yet interconnected with the other parts (1 Corinthians 12:12). No one part of the body can say to another "I don't need you" or "I have nothing to contribute (1 Corinthians 12:15-27). In that same context Paul, makes it clear that God has given each person certain spiritual gifts to contribute to the whole body and that "to each one the manifestation of the Spirit is given for the common good" (1 Corinthians 12:7). In Israel, the distinctive contributions were more focused on the tribes and the role they played, but in the New Covenant the Spirit is given to every believer that they would be gifted and empowered to serve God's people in a unique and important way.

5. To Contribute To God's Work

Nehemiah 10:35, "We also assume responsibility for bringing to the house of the LORD each year the firstfruits of our crops and of every fruit tree.

Nehemiah 10:39, "We will not neglect the house of our God."

The contributions that God's people were to make were not just in the form of how they could serve; they were also in the form of the financial provision necessary for God to be worshiped in the way that He desired. This meant making sure that financial provision was made for the full-time workers in God's House. Everyone had a responsibility to make sure that a tithe of their money and goods was brought in so that all the adequate supplies could be purchased and the Levites (who worked at the Temple and supported its activities) were properly provided for. The temple was not viewed as "the priests'"; everyone in this covenant renewal took responsibility for the house of God, to make sure it was not neglected.

Again, as we arrive in the New Covenant, there are differences and similarities to what we encounter here. The main difference is that now the temple is not the building but the people, individually and corporately (1 Corinthians 3:16, 6:19). But God's people are still encouraged to take ownership of that temple, the church, and ensure that it is properly provided for (including making provision for those whose vocational work serves the church (1 Timothy 5:17-18; 1 Corinthians 9:7-11). We still do well to embrace the mentality that one Bible scholar says marked the Jewish approach to giving: "The grace of giving—giving to the Lord's house—was a mark of piety and devotion. It was *sacrificial* giving. The *firstfruits* were the choicest, and in giving them to the Lord's house the Jews signaled the principle that 'God comes first.'"[15] Indeed, when our mindset is one of "God comes first," commitment to holiness should be the result in every arena of life, including what we do with our time and where we invest our finances.

Next Steps

So, how can we stay committed to the pathway of rebuilt lives in a way that the Israelites of Nehemiah 13 did not? It won't be easy. As we have acknowledged, commitments are tough to keep. We as people are not good at keeping oaths. We know that phrase "sometime later" is a commitment killer. The age-old statement is that "time heals all wounds," and while it may do that, it certainly

---

15   Thomas, 371-372.

doesn't tend to do a lot for commitments. Just think about the oaths taken every new year and what things look like in March. The full gyms and new gym memberships every January are almost always wiped out by April. We obviously need pathways for staying committed, things that help us avoid the backsliding that we see so clearly portrayed here.

One of them is to reflect on the dangers of what happens when you do not stay committed to God and His Word. If we do not stay committed,

1. **Old enemies return.** Nehemiah learned that Tobiah (remember him) was being rented a room in the temple structure! For us, these old enemies are old sins, old habits that come back easily when we give up the commitments we want to maintain for the Lord.

2. **God's house is neglected.** Nehemiah learned that the provision assigned to the Levites had not been given to them, and that all the Levites and musicians responsible for the service had gone back to their own fields. For us we must remember to keep Matthew 6:19-21 in mind about laying up treasures on earth where moth and rust destroy.

3. **Our worship falters.** Nehemiah found that people were treading the winepress and buying grain on the Sabbath, old patterns returned of doing business that compromised the Sabbath as a day set aside for worship. For us, we must ask whether we also allow business practices and the way of the world to invade how we spend Sunday as the Lord's day.

4. **Our lives suffer.** Nehemiah insisted that it was because of marriages like Solomon's (who married foreign women) that Israel sinned so grievously and suffered the

punishment of God's rebuke. Solomon stands as a warning of a life that started well (he was the wisest king to ever live) but declined because the inevitable creep of worldly pleasures and desires caused his life to suffer. We too must be aware of the fact that sin comes with consequences. We reap what we sow, which should give us pause before we simply give up on the path of staying committed to God and His ways.

So, how is it any different for us than it was for the people in Nehemiah's day? Aren't we doomed to repeat their sad history, one of starting with high hopes and grand aspirations but ending in failure and abandoned commitments? The short answer is no. Though we want to be aware that we face similar dangers and temptations as them, it doesn't have to be that way. There is another path, the path of staying faithful to the covenant commitments that God's people have made. It is a path that is open to us because of something that happens a little over four hundred years after Nehemiah's time.

Significantly, the book of Nehemiah is the last part of the historical books of the Old Testament to be recorded. It is the last thing officially on the page until the coming of John the Baptist. It rings again and again over that four hundred years about the fickleness of the people of God. For all of Nehemiah's reforming efforts, for all the miraculous achievements of a rebuilt wall and a reconstituted people under God's Word, the people don't see their commitments through. But this was all preparing the way for the greater Nehemiah, for the true Israelite who never broke his commitments but saw them through to the very end.

Jesus Christ was obedient until the point of death (Philippians 2:8). He is called Faithful and True (Revelation 19:11). Though we are prone to wander and stray, Jesus Christ is the

Rock Who dies in our place for the forgiveness of our sins. Jesus solves our "commitment issues" by committing to the Father and to us, in His life, death on the cross, and resurrection. And He has given us the power of the Holy Spirit so that we can follow Him in staying the course. Of course, there will still be challenges. But now we know we have it in us to overcome those challenges and continue the work of rebuilding our lives as the Lord enables by His Spirit.

So, I want to close by encouraging you to pause and prayerfully, solemnly determine what you believe the Lord wants you to commit to as a next step of following Him and ensuring that you and your family are seeking to fulfill His will and plan for your lives. In order to have lasting results, in order for true reform and revival and lasting life change to occur, it takes a process of committing again and again when we have failed, renewing our commitment to maintain the priorities the Lord has for us.

Yes, it will be hard work. But the Lord promises to be with you in it. And you are not alone: everyone who is a part of His church is undergoing the same challenge and relying on God's grace and the encouragement of the community for it. Because of what Christ has done and because of the Spirit's power at work within me, I know I can grow in staying committed. It will require hard work. It will require community. It will require accountability. But, as Max Lucado has stated, "God never said that the journey would be easy, but He did say that the arrival would be worthwhile."

Prayer: Heavenly Father, thank You for leading me through this study of the portion of Your Word known as Nehemiah. I pray You could continue to do the good work in me that You intend Your Word to do: transforming me into a person who can keep our commitments to You because of Your grace and power working through me. Help me to take the next step of faith, whatever that looks like. And may I keep my eyes firmly fixed on Christ, the author and perfecter of my faith. It is in His mighty name I pray...Amen.

Conclusion

Committing to Commitments:

We have seen in the book of Nehemiah how the Lord was faithful to his people even amidst their failures and shortcomings. We have seen how the Lord raised up Nehemiah to spearhead a vital rebuilding effort, and how the story of rebuilding Jerusalem's walls is a picture of the rebuilding that needs to occur in our own lives and our own world. We have seen how it is vital in this rebuilding effort to know the vision God has for your life, to know your place among God's people, to know the mission God has given to the church, to face the opposition that will inevitably arise, to maintain your focus on who God wants us to be, and to stay committed to the work the Lord has given us to do. And we have seen that when we fail to do these various things, God is faithful to sustain us and set us back on the proper track of rebuilding our lives.

And now, at the end of our study, I want to spend some time thinking a little bit more about the importance of commitments. It would be so easy to finish this book and say, "Wow, I can't wait to rebuild my life!" and then walk out the door *and absolutely nothing about your life changes.* Why? Because you are essentially living your life by default rather than by design. What do I mean by that? Well, I mean that all of us tend to live our lives *defaulting* to the old patterns and old ways of doing things unless we make intentional commitments that help us fight against those default patterns and live in a way that conforms to God's design for our lives. If you have poor spending habits that have developed over years and years, you can't just *read a book* about becoming more financially responsible; you have to make a commitment to living in ways that will slowly but surely lead to changes in your life. In short, commitments are key to genuine life change; they are essential to seeing that rebuilding efforts do not just peter out like typical new year's resolutions, but instead go the distance.

There are lots of reasons people give for why they don't want to make commitments. Many people experiencing what has been referred to as "decision fatigue" just do not want to make any more decisions, especially if they involve long term commitments. The problem here is that by deciding not to make any decisions...they have decided. By not making a commitment, they have made a commitment to the default ways of their old life. The reality is, we make decisions, and thus commitments, all the time. The question is: what sorts of decisions and commitments are we making, and do they align with God's vision for our lives?

For others, making a commitment or multiple commitments just isn't appealing: why tie yourself down in any way and hinder your freedom to live in the moment? The fact that there is an increase in the divorce rate and couples that are living together is just one example of how much our society increasingly sees commitment as passé. But in actuality, committing yourself to the kinds of patterns that help us live the life God has designed for us is the way to true freedom. True freedom is living in the way

God has intended, not being a slave to sin and our fleshly desires. Commitments can be one of the strongest things that helps us live into that freedom.

Still others of you are saying: "I've made commitments before, and they've always failed. Why would anything be different this time? This is an important objection to address, particularly because it is so common and so powerful. I would say this objection is one of the strongest tools the Enemy has to try and short circuit change in the Christian life, trying to convince us to give up: we've failed in the past, so we'll fail again in the future. But this is where we need to fight with the logic of grace! All of us *have failed*, and that is why we needed God's undeserved favor shown in Christ. And all of us *fail*, and yet we know God sustains us through those failures and calls us to carry on. If you have failed in carrying through a commitment made in the past...welcome to the club! All of God's people are in that same boat, and that can be important motivation for us to know that hope is not lost: by God's grace, this next commitment is one that you can see through by God's power at work anew in your life.

We cannot let these objections to commitments (and others) win out, because making commitments that matter is the key to rebuilding lives that matter. If we do not make the right commitments or if we don't make commitments at all, we will be living lives that don't align with God's best for us. In fact, making long-term commitments is one of the most important ways that we will overcome short-term setbacks. We all have setbacks in rebuilding lives that matter; the question is, how do we respond when we encounter them? Commitments give us additional motivation at just the right time: when we are tempted to throw in the towel. Commitments are ultimately what lead to true, lasting change; it is the *commitment* to a healthier lifestyle that enables someone to lose weight and get more exercise; it is that same *commitment* that helps them get back on track after a day, or week, or month of unhealthy eating habits. It is commitment that shapes our character and that ultimately enables the rewards of a changed live to be achieved.

What Sorts of Commitments Are Needed to Rebuild?

So, if we are going to rebuild by God's grace, what sort of commitments should we consider? Commitments that honor the Lord, that stretch our faith, and that help us press into the community of believers. God rewards these sorts of commitments because they help us focus on what really matters. They enable our lives to become effective and productive both physically and spiritually. They are key to rebuilding a life that matters.

While there are many such commitments, let me just share four with you here that I think are particularly significant to rebuilding lives that matter.

#1: Commit to Worship: One of the best things you can do in your life is to make a weekly commitment to be with God's people in corporate worship. Nothing can refresh a person more than coming to worship and lifting one's voice to the Creator of the universe and let the worries of the world fade away. If you find yourself spiritually and physically exhausted, if you feel like you can't go on, if you think the rebuilding effort is hopeless, then you need God to empower and energize you for the days ahead, and corporate worship is the primary place the Lord does this.

#2: Commit to Reading God's Word: Just as we need worship to inspire and empower us, we need God's Word to instruct us. This world is constantly trying to steer us in the wrong direction or push us toward decisions that keep us from attaining God's best in our lives. Our best response is to read and meditate on God's Word daily. All through Scripture, we are told that the

reading of God's Word is vital to staying on track with the rebuilding effort; it is the guiding light for our path in an oftentimes dark world.

#3: Commit to a Small Group: Just like I need worship to inspire me and God's Word to instruct me, I need God's people to support, encourage and pray for me. God created us as relational beings and we need the strength a small group brings. We have so much we have been called to do in this world, but we were never called to do it alone. A small group community that knows you and can support you when you are down (and where you can support others when they are down) is vital the rebuilding effort, especially because they can keep you accountable to the commitments that you make!

#4: Commit to Serve in Your Local Church: God has made it so that we need to serve in order to flex and grow our spiritual muscles; in other words, serving is crucial to growth in the Christian life. God created us for good works (Ephesians 2:10), and when we all serve together great things happen. In Nehemiah's day, it was rebuilding a wall; in the era of the church, we have clear instruction that we are to serve in the local church. There are many great charitable organizations out there to serve, and many needy people to come alongside. But serving the Body of Christ is a top priority of the Christian life. When God's children make a commitment to serve alongside each other in their local church, miracles happen, and the work of rebuilding continues.

So, I want to encourage you to take some time and consider which of these four commitments the Spirit of God might be calling you to make at this time...perhaps it is all of them! As you pray about this, may I encourage you to go way out on a limb in making these commitments? Why go out on a limb? Because that is where the fruit of personal change is found. Commitments enable us to join the same rebuilding effort that Nehemiah was a part of so many years ago, rebuilding the lives of God's people from the rubble of their failures so that they can live as God intended, for the life of the world, the good of the church, and the glory of God.